THE TUNNEL AT THE END OF THE LIGHT

UNITING THE EUROPEAN ECONOMY

A BRIE/Kreisky Forum Project

The Tunnel at the End of the Light: Privatization, Business Networks, and Economic Transformation in Russia

Stephen S. Cohen, Andrew Schwartz, and John Zysman, Editors

Enlarging Europe: The Industrial Foundations of a New Political Reality

John Zysman and Andrew Schwartz, Editors

RESEARCH SERIES / NUMBER 100

THE TUNNEL AT THE END OF THE LIGHT:

PRIVATIZATION, BUSINESS NETWORKS, AND ECONOMIC TRANSFORMATION IN RUSSIA

Stephen S. Cohen, Andrew Schwartz, and John Zysman, Editors

A BRIE/KREISKY FORUM PROJECT

IAS
International
and Area Studies

UNIVERSITY OF CALIFORNIA AT BERKELEY

Library of Congress Cataloging-in-Publication Data

The tunnel at the end of the light : privatization, business networks, and economic transformation in Russia / Stephen S. Cohen, Andrew Schwartz, and John Zysman, editors.
p. cm. — (Research series ; no. 100)
"A BRIE/Kreisky Forum Project".
Includes bibliographical references.
ISBN 0-87725-000-6 (pbk.)
1. Russia (Federation)—Economic conditions—1991- 2. Business networks—Russia (Federation) 3. Commercial crimes—Russia (Federation) 4. Informal sector (Economics)—Russia (Federation) 5. Post-communism—Russia (Federation) 6. Russia (Federation)—Social conditions—1991- 7. Russia (Federation)—Foreign economic relations. I. Cohen, Stephen S. II. Schwartz, Andrew, 1957- . III. Zysman, John. IV. BRIE/Kreisky Forum Project. V. Series: Research series (University of California, Berkeley. International and Area Studies) ; no. 100.
HC340.12.T86 1998
338.947—dc21

98-34006
CIP

Printed in the United States of America

CONTENTS

PREFACE AND ACKNOWLEDGMENTS

This volume's title and main argument first appeared in an essay by Stephen S. Cohen and Andrew Schwartz in 1992—a fact underscored to suggest the current Russian situation's predictability.[1] The volume is one of two emerging from a BRIE/Kreisky Forum project on the reintegration of industrial Europe—of the market economies in the West with the command economies of the East. The project has examined the role of international production networks (IPNs) in generating an integrated production system in the European region. Our findings indicate that, with the exception of Russia, IPNs are increasingly significant in a range of industries from electronics through textiles. They involve much more than just the substitution of cheap Eastern labor for more expensive Western labor, or a migration of plant instead of people. Rather they constitute an increasingly complex reorganization of production that can advance the competitiveness of companies throughout Europe.

The bulk of the project work, published as *Enlarging Europe: The Industrial Foundations of a New Political Reality,* focused on the Central European economies as the primary sources for the emerging network nodes.[2] We did not originally intend to produce a separate volume on the post-Communist Russian economy. But of course the Central European countries are relatively small. In Asia, where IPNs already play a transformative role, the population totals are an order of magnitude larger. Indeed the Asian supply of IPNs is now, with China's reforms and its entry into the world trading system, effectively unlimited. The European analog to East Asia, and especially to China, is Russia, suggesting the comparative question, "What role would Russia play in Europe's emerging production networks?" With the cooperation of a wide range of colleagues in Europe and the United States, we set out to explore this question. The answer, and the dismal evidence presented in this volume, is that the Russian transition has spawned an abundance of networks, predatory and survivalist, but few to date that actively participate in IPNs or hold promise for any productive role in European integration. That result, which proved both too significant and too troublesome to be adequately treated in *Enlarging Europe*, is argued out in this book.

The undertaking and completion of this project has depended heavily on the support and cooperation of a very diverse group of colleagues and supporters. Our deepest debt is to Professor Oliver Rathkolb, research coordinator, and Margit Schmidt, secretary general, of the Kreisky Forum for International Dialogue. Together they helped both orchestrate the conversations on which this project has rested and arrange the funding that made them possible. Their confidence and support were indispensable and highly valued. Professor Rathkolb, himself a fine historian of contemporary Europe who prepared Bruno Kreisky's memoirs, has become a good friend and intellectual colleague. Our debt to him cannot be fully expressed. The support of the Austrian government, particularly the Federal Chancellery, including Ulrich Stacher, head of department, and his collaborator, Maria Leitgeb, has also been crucial. The president of the Bruno Kreisky Forum, former chancellor Franz Vranitsky, both participated in our meetings and extended strong support.

The funding required to bring this work to a broader public audience has been provided by the German Marshall Fund of the United States, the Copenhagen Business School (CBS), and the World Bank. At the German Marshall Fund Craig Kennedy and Andrea Essler supported the project. Further financial and intellectual backing came from the CBS as part of an ongoing collaboration with UC Berkeley. Our work with Niels Mygind, director of the Center for East European Studies at CBS, has added a Baltic perspective to the undertaking. The Economic Development Institute at the World Bank provided both intellectual support and financial assistance. At the Bank David Ellerman first took an interest in this effort, along with Xavier Simon, then chief of the Finance and Industry Division. When Xavier Simon stepped down because of illness, his engagement was maintained by Danny Leipziger, whose work on economic development itself contributed to our thinking. Funding for the underlying intellectual work on production networks has been provided to BRIE by the Alfred P. Sloan Foundation; President Ralph Gomery and Vice-President Hirsch Cohen have been strong forces in shaping that effort. Other research funding was provided by the University of California's Center for German and European Studies, whose director, Professor Gerald D. Feldman, and executive director, Beverly K. Crawford, provided assistance.

Many others have provided substantive intellectual support and support for the questions we are asking. Professor André Sapir, president of the Institut d'Études Européennes at the Université Libre de Bruxelles, was an early participant in the discussions leading to this project. The project's original formulation as a study of foreign direct investment in Eastern Europe was written with Laura d'Andrea Tyson before she went to Washington to serve as chair of the Council of Economic Advisors. At the European Commission Stefano Micossi, director general of DG III, has been a constant source of ideas and discussion. Galway Johnson, head of unit, Information Technologies Industries in DG III, encouraged us by insisting that network phenomena were emerging in the European electronics sector. Harald Johansen, vice president of Supply and Distribution of Ericsson; Hans J. Pedersen, vice president of Danfoss; and Humphrey Porter, managing director of Neutronics, likewise provided insight into emerging business networks. A number of colleagues and collaborators offered significant commentary, helpful suggestions, and incisive criticisms of the papers presented at the conferences held at the CBS in October 1996 and at the Kreisky Forum for International Dialogue in June 1997. They include: Jan Annerstedt, Vladimir Dimovski, Eileen Doherty, Gabriel Eichler, Dennis Encarnation, Dieter Ernst, Stephan Haggard, Attila Havas, Joel Hellman, Finn Junge-Jensen, Brian Kick, Bengt-Åke Lundvall, Snejina Mihaylova, Stefano Micossi, Jan Mladek, Julie Pellegrin, Peter Petri, André Sapir, Károly Attila Soós, Sam Steffensen, Richard Steinberg, Lauge Stetting, Tim Sturgeon, Márton Szabó, Jan Turcan, Dean White, and Matt Zook.

The staffs of BRIE, the CBS, and the Kreisky Forum all contributed to the conferences and the meetings. Eureka Endo and Patricia Johnson wrote substantial portions of the briefing books for these two meetings. Their work was of the highest quality. Without their help, those meetings could not have happened. At BRIE, Patricia Johnson participated patiently in the evolution of the undertaking. Dan Adler and Cynthia Berg made major contributions as the project emerged. Cynthia Berg also made substantial intellectual contributions to several of the chapters. Marybeth Schubert and Ann Mine have facilitated the entire effort. At the CBS, Karen Bjerre did the meeting planning and Professor Sam Steffensen worked with us to make that session possible and to facilitate our discussions in Denmark. In Vienna, Karin Mendel and Melitta Campostrini of the Kreisky Forum, as well as Stefan August Lütengau and Ingeborg Hausknost of the Kreisky Archives, made arrangements for our second session.

The shaping of this material into a book required an exceptional effort. Dr. Paul M. Pitman, an historian, made deeply appreciated substantive and editorial contributions. David Szanton and the staff of International and Area Studies Publications at the University of California, Berkeley have done a remarkable job in both preparing the complex manuscript and assuring it would be ready for the meetings hosted by the Austrian Chancellery.

NOTES

1. Stephen S. Cohen and Andrew Schwartz, "The Tunnel at the End of the Light" (Berkeley: Berkeley Roundtable on the International Economy [BRIE], University of California, September 1992); BRIE Working Paper No. 56; republished in *American Prospect*, no. 13 (Spring 1993) and in Russian in *EKO* 9, 231 and 10, 232 (1993).
2. See John Zysman and Andrew Schwartz, eds., *Enlarging Europe: The Industrial Foundations of a New Political Reality* (Berkeley: International and Area Studies, 1998), a summary of which is provided in the appendix of this volume.

DEEPER INTO THE TUNNEL[1]

Stephen S. Cohen and Andrew Schwartz

The collapse of the Soviet regime opened the way for the eager construction of a new Russia to be built on the pillars of political democracy, a market economy, and an open society. The results are proving to be disastrous. Since 1989 every economic and social indicator has fallen—except one: the ratio of exports to GNP rose because GNP fell faster than exports.[2] And all these indicators did not just fall once in a big bang and then begin to recover; they fell year upon year, compounding away along a downward trajectory that has yet to reverse.

The data themselves are as rotten as the situation they portray and should be taken, therefore, not as fodder for econometric exercises, but as faulty indicators of a deeply flawed economic/social situation—rather like the pixels on a display screen; enough of them, despite their imperfections and the gaps between them, convey to your mind the wherewithal to form a picture. One rather well-known picture is suggested: Ambrogio Lorenzetti's Renaissance mural in the Sienna Town Hall depicting *The Allegory of Good and Bad Government,* whose parts juxtapose a utopian portrait of civic life, commerce, and agriculture with an instructive image of tyranny, greed, and corruption.

Russia's GNP is now about half its 1989 level. The descent has been persistent: 1991 GNP was down 5 percent on 1990; 1992 down 19 percent on 1991; 1993 down 12 percent on 1992; 1994 down 13 percent on 1993; 1995 down 4 percent on 1994; and despite upbeat forecasts during the 1996 election campaign, 1996 was down 6 percent on 1995.[3] Estimates of real wages, taken independently of these GNP estimates, show average real wages to be down about half.[4] Even electricity production (taken by many as a more robust economic indicator than GNP, wages, and employment-type statistics) evidences a steady and continuing decline: it has gone down in every year through the first half of 1997 for a cumulative drop of about one-fourth.[5]

Foreign direct investment (FDI), which was supposed to be a major motor of Russian economic reform and reinvigoration, has proven thus far to be a tragic cargo cult; it never materialized. Amounts have been trivial; they are not yet increasing. The few individual cases, such as IBM,[6] reveal not the travails of a promising start but the kind of immuno-rejection effects of systemic pathology. Any comparison with China is so unflattering as to border on poor taste. The most upbeat official FDI figures for Russia count $12 billion cumulative through 1996, while China received $34 billion in 1994, $36 billion in 1995, and $40 billion in 1996.[7]

Rather than benefiting from an inflow of foreign capital—the premise and promise of the radical reformers—Russia has been a net capital exporter: Manuel Castells cites estimates of $60 billion, but reliable estimates are hard to come by as most of the money is neither scrupulously recorded nor terribly "clean." The biggest flows of foreign capital have not been FDI—which brings technology, knowhow, network connections, etc. with it—but rather portfolio investment, which brings just itself, for as long as it stays, plus a few yuppies to set styles of conspicuous consumption for the new moneyed elite in Moscow. The flow of funds has been directed at the Russian stock and debt markets and is highly liquid, nervous money seeking speculative gains from bargain-priced assets in oil, gas, nickel, and electricity generation. This "hot" money can leave as quickly as it arrived and bequeath a legacy of discredited markets and a fragile currency. Little of the foreign inflow is aimed at, or is going into, real investment—i.e., the act that gives capitalism its ultimate legitimacy: putting capital into well-chosen tools to produce the right things. Data are lacking, but there is no hint of positive industrial investment in Russia; there are, however, abundant indications of serious disinvestment (as in declining oil and gas production and delivery as the system decays).

Finally, social indicators flash a comparably tragic picture: life expectancy has fallen dramatically as crude death rates soared.[8] Even murder rates have soared, catapulting Russia to the top of the charts of "high homicide countries."[9] Income distribution rapidly shifted as resources were concentrated in an astonishingly small proportion of the population (mostly in Moscow and a few other urban centers), so that some folks grew truly rich by world standards while the majority of the population grew poorer—so much poorer that meat and milk consumption fell substantially and the proportion of the population living "in poverty" (measured the "tough love" way—i.e., as food consumption needed to maintain body weight) rose to over one-third.[10]

This appalling trajectory is not the result of accident or external events. It is the inevitable consequence of analysis and choice that ignore a market economy's critical institutional need for clear and enforced rules—that is, for a functioning, competent public administration. Stock ownership comes second, a distant second. In Russia, it was the starting point—and ending point—for the radical privatizers. The early choices of the radical privatizers yielded their dire consequences, as the one reinforced the other in a downward spiral, pushing Russia into an economic, political and, crucially, social vortex. Creating a market-driven economy (and a political democracy) is not just about dismantling state regulations, controls, and capacity for action, distributing shares in giant monopolies, and running elections. It is, first, about building institutions. And the core of the Russian failure is in institution building, especially the key institution, a functioning state. As we have argued, "The creation of an honest and effective public administration—not the broad distribution of shares in uncompetitive giant firms—is the key step toward the creation of a successful capitalist market system and a functioning democracy."[11]

The Soviet totalitarian state was a horror; the danger of its reviving itself was incentive enough for its speedy and complete destruction. But too little attention was paid to the compelling need to create an effective public administration and a credible rule of law. An institutional vacuum is not an intelligent successor regime to a totalitarian police state; it is a formula for danger. The dismantled public administration has been unable to set out laws, rules, and regulations and to enforce them. Nor has it been able to provide the assurance that contracts are enforceable. It has not even been able to provide basic police protection, without which there can be no real investment, no normal business operation, no effective civil liberty. Instead, Russia has become a criminalized society. Privatization of big enterprises has generated not a surge in private investment, but the looting of public assets. Instead of removing the old nomenklatura from power, Russia now has nomenklatura capitalism. Instead of a burgeoning class of small capitalists, there is a class of big gangsters. In place of taxes there are shakedowns. In brief, though there are markets and an active stock exchange and elections, there is neither capitalism nor democracy.

II

The choices of the radical privatizers rested on a very particular theory of economy and politics in which the mere fact of private property would generate functioning markets and liberal politics.[12] That theory, or what we label *neo-liberalism*, presented both a call to action and an internally consistent set of propositions that need to be reviewed before evaluating its impact in Russia.

Privatization—the process which transfers state-owned assets to private owners—has been the core policy of economic liberalization in Russia. Russian reformers (and their Western advisers) presumed that private owners are at once the basis for a market economy and democracy and the main instrument to break the economic and political power of the state. According to neo-liberals, privatization is the bridge from communism to capitalism. Two prominent neo-liberals, Graham Allison and Grigory Yavlinsky, wrote in 1991:

> In economics, the core value of freedom is exercised in a *market economy* based on private ownership in which market forces of supply and demand answer the question of who produces what for whom. . . . Ownership means the freedom to use and dispose of property as an individual chooses. Basic laws of economics tolerate no equivocation on this point, none whatsoever.[13]

The immediate neo-liberal objective of privatization is to create first private owners, not just private owners. This distinction stresses that the first private owners created by privatization are temporary owners; it is the "last" owners who will restructure companies and lead the move to democracy. The first ownership structure is then an artifact of privatization, but little more.[14]

Market logic in a system of private ownership automatically will create the active private owners that enable free markets to produce prosperity and democracy. First private owners sell to intermediate private owners—an optional step—who then sell to active private owners. Neo-liberals pay no attention to the market experience, skills, or attitudes of the first owners. They contend that the first owners, whoever they were, would be "economic" men, though they had lived under a state socialist system for decades.[15] Neo-liberals only disdain first owners, such as workers, who would have "obvious" nonmarket incentives in a market economy.[16] The "last" owners are active private owners, who pay the highest prices for assets because they can extract the most value from them.

Moreover, a private ownership system presumably solves the transaction cost problem concerning the protection of private property and the lack of reliable market rules. First owners could get the maximum prices for their assets only if the active owners knew that property rights were secure—that is, if reliable rules were in place. Therefore, first owners have incentives to create and enforce laws and procedures that protect private property. In these ways, a private ownership system establishes an efficient market economy and a modern democracy. Privatization's clear logic and clarity of purpose focuses reformers on the task at hand: how to privatize.

Luckily, the transition's political opportunities had offered the Russian reformers a historic chance to privatize. They could act before privatization's likely opponents, who were momentarily disoriented by the Communist system's collapse, could respond. Reformers risked a return to the Communist past or an unthinkable move backward to the Third World by delaying privatization or, worse, by failing to privatize altogether. The neo-liberal solution was then obvious: not just privatization, but *rapid* privatization.

We contend below that neo-liberal theory, which derives its intellectual power from its narrow assumptions, neglected the real world possibility that once established, the Russian first private owners might hijack the system, which, as we all know, indeed happened. Moreover, we contend that this eventuality was predictable and perhaps preventable .

The dismal alliterative, "foreseen, forlorn, and forbidding," summarizes the consequences of the radical privatization program. Neither accident, external circumstance, nor error of execution intervened to fundamentally shape outcomes. They were foreseeable, if not in extent, at least in terms of cause and direction. The cause was the complete failure of the radical privatizers to understand that the creation of an effective public administration, the most important of capitalism's retaining walls—and not the rapid distribution and trading of ownership shares in uncompetitive giant firms—is the necessary precondition for the creation of a successful capitalistic market system and a functioning democracy. The task was institution building; the necessary intellectual approach, institutional. In the event, institutional thinking was ignored; so too were its conclusions.

We wrote the paragraphs in the following section in 1991; they were published the following year.[17] They present what at the time was considered an excessively gloomy prognosis for the results of Russia's radical privatization. Perhaps it was not sufficiently pessimistic.

III

In the former Soviet empire, the collapse of communism created an opportunity for the victims of one failed utopian ideology to find another. The evaporating Soviet system left an ideological vacuum that was quickly filled as legions of Western advisers arrived to help translate the goals of political democracy and a market economy into an action agenda: "democracy" translated quickly into elections; "a market economy," into privatization.

As in many hurried translations, the bare essentials were grasped, but much was missed. Elections are essential to democracy, but functioning democracies are built on much more than just elections. And private ownership, especially of shares of very large enterprises, is only one element of a modern market economy. But it was fundamentalist capitalism that poured in—the simple, universal program that all could understand: free prices, free trade, and, above all, privatize.

The fate of small enterprises like shops, restaurants, or farms was never at issue. Everyone agreed that rapid small-scale privatization was the best way to energize private sector growth and to develop a capitalist ethic and an entrepreneurial class.

The thornier question was how, and how fast, to privatize the clunking state enterprises that employed thousands and thousands. Supposedly, only an abrupt and ruthless privatization could clear the stage of the remnants of a command economy—the perverse incentives, the incompetent and corrupt apparatchiks, the endless subsidies, the mindless production of the wrong goods. Delay risked permitting those who stood to lose the most from privitization—the old line bureaucrats and the managers and workers of the giant state enterprises—to undermine the privitization process, thereby jeopardizing the transition to a market economy. According to Harvard University economist Jeffery Sachs,

> The need to accelerate privatization is the paramount economic policy issue. If there is no breakthrough in privatization in large enterprises in the near future, the entire process could be stalled for political and social reasons for years to come, with dire consequences.[18]

The Economist agreed, calling "the growing acceptance of . . . gradualism . . . the greatest peril."[19]

But there is an alternative to radical privatization, and it is not just a smokescreen put forward by nostalgics for the old system. It is the safest and sanest approach to building a market economy and democratic society.

Rapid privatization will backfire, for few of the newly privatized big companies can survive in a competitive market environment. The structures of both supply and demand for these giant firms have been shattered; the industrial linkages are severed. The abrupt political change separated enterprises from their traditional customers the way the movement of rivers into new channels left medieval entrepot towns high and dry on silted streams. The economic collapse resulting from sudden privatization would result in extensive layoffs, massive bankruptcies, and, ultimately, social unrest. In a climate of chaos, the state would eventually have to support the failing enterprises, one way or another.

Markets cannot regulate monopolies. A heritage of monopolies implies active regulation. Who shall regulate monopoly and oligopoly industries? Who shall oversee the liquidation of the losers, the temporary subsidy of restructurings, and the reemployment of workers? For a prolonged period, newly privatized firms will not be able to compete in their home markets against superior imported goods. Who shall oversee international trade and ration foreign exchange, as West European governments had to do after World War II? Further, such essential preconditions for modern capitalist economies as an established legal system or tax code, financial institutions, and effective capital markets do not yet exist. These shortcomings increase the odds that a "big bang privatization" will turn into a "big bust."

This essay develops the argument for a pragmatic approach to privatization. It boils down to three basic contentions.

First, privatizing ownership will not by itself make large, uncompetitive enterprises operate efficiently. Nor will distributing share ownership in those companies create a market system or a capitalist culture.

Second, private ownership makes sense only in the context of embedded socioeconomic institutions. Big companies do not exist in an institutional vacuum. Nor do markets. Both require external structures of law, finance, and regulation. Erecting a system of domestic finance with efficient capital markets is but one important example of such needed institutions.

Third, the state will inevitably play the major role in industrial development, for a long interim. It will help create and regulate markets; it will control imports and oversee the flow of capital; and, irrespective of the chosen privatization strategy, it will effectively control substantial portions of major industrial assets . The competitive vulnerability of existing industry allows no other alternative for the near future. *The creation of an honest and effective public administration—not the broad distribution of shares in uncompetitive giant firms—is the key step toward the creation of a successful capitalistic market system and a functioning democracy.*

THE VARIETIES OF CAPITALIST EXPERIENCE, OR WHO OWNS MITSUBISHI?

Radical capitalists ignore the great differences in the institutions of private ownership of big firms in such successful capitalist countries as the United States, Japan, Germany, France, and Italy, as well as the other enormous institutional differences that distinguish the competing capitalisms. They strip away the complex variety and reduce private ownership to the simple model of textbook economics. They neglect history; they discard experience. Any remotely appropriate historical experience—such as Europe after World War I or World War II—points in a quite different direction.

Radical capitalists insist that only a system of privately owned firms linked together by markets provides the right incentives and the right constraints, a set of signals that promotes social dynamism and optimal allocation. Moreover, market signals are prompt and unrelenting. Adaptation is fast and permanent. One of the impressive aesthetics of capitalism is the perfect match between efficiency in capital formation and efficiency in production. Moreover, newly privatized industries are likely to attract foreign investors—the main sources of modern technology and management skills—more readily than state counterparts. Finally, competition will relentlessly downsize the old industrial monsters into more productively sized companies.

At first glance, the radical capitalist argument is appealing. The problem is, of course, that the textbook caricatures of the institutions of modern capitalism obscure an understanding of how the different systems actually function. Take the two critical institutions—price-driven, "free" capital markets and private ownership of giant corporations. Neither is simple in practice, and neither is universal in form.

In France, as in Japan, and also in Germany and Korea, for more than a generation after World War II, capital markets were neither "free" nor price-driven. To a critical extent, especially where giant corporations were concerned, capital was allocated administratively, less by price (as in the proposed capital markets for the ex-Soviet empire) than by administrative systems of priorities.

Nor does the pragmatic experience of forms of ownership correspond to the simplistic radical capitalist model. In Japan, the most successful case ever of rapid development, ownership is "private," but only if one defines "private" as not owned by the state. Interlocking shareholding and finance within *keiretsu* created something far removed from the simple ownership model of the radical capitalists. Keiretsu have no obvious analogy in the rest of the First World and no place whatever in Econ 101 textbooks. Who owns Mitsubishi? Perhaps the most accurate functional answer is "Mitsubishi owns Mitsubishi."

The form of ownership is an important element in modern capitalism, but it is less a unifying than a differentiating characteristic, and it takes its real world meaning only within the complex institutional context that defines a particular capitalist system. There is more than one variety of successful capitalism.

STRUCTURAL CONSTRAINTS AND REALISTIC CHOICES

The Communist system left a legacy which will shape the results of privatization.

Shortage of entrepreneurial experience; surplus of criminal experience. Communism has produced a managerial class ill-equipped to function in a capitalist market. The best of the technical-managerial leadership is lodged in the declining military-industrial complex, a declining market. Most of the market experience comes from the "second economy," and it is dubious that such experience will translate into competent large company ownership or management.

Besides the petty black marketeers, the other likely new ownership stratum is those who made money illegally—big-time black marketeers or corrupt bureaucrats—or both working together, as they always have. They are best positioned to cash in on abrupt privatizations. They can split enterprises into valuable and potentially negative parts, shift labor across those parts, maintain control of the good bits, and reap a capital gain at the moment of privatization—millionaires in one quick shot. They can reap a windfall gain no matter how the enterprise performs. Even where assets are auctioned to the highest bidder, these networks of officials and plant managers, with their underground allies (most often called, locally, "the Mafia"), typically have the cash and insider knowledge to bid. This potential was not lost on sophisticated foreign advisers: bars in foreigners-only hotels are filled with IMF and World Bank officials explaining how the late medieval capitalists in Europe were considered, in their time, to be criminal elements. Likewise, the winners of the American bootlegging wars have now become solid corporate capitalists. Privatization ideally would transform the criminal mafias into normal organizations—unless, of course, the Southern Italian model were to prevail.

Shortage of companies ready for a market economy. Most of the giant enterprises are burdened with obsolete product and process technology and mountains of debt. The debt will be written off by the state one way or another. But even with newly cleaned balance sheets, they are poor candidates for market viability. Finding real private owners to run them, without permanent subsidy and protection, will be difficult.

Shortage of domestic and international capital. The newly privatized firms, striving to become competitive, will not be the only large claimants on the small capital pool. Indeed, they will most likely find themselves at the end of the queue. The best candidates for privatization, and for capital infusions, are the classic infrastructural industries: telecommunications; roadbuilding; railways; airlines; and oil, gas, nickel, aluminum, and the like, not to mention the special case of electric power generation—the handling of those dangerous nuclear power plants on Europe's doorstep. The West Europeans want those stations rebuilt for safety, and their nuclear power industry is hurting from a lack of orders. They will provide massive investment to the newly privatizing electric utilities, thus combining safety and capitalist development in the East along with safety and the generation of business for state supported industry in the West.

Privatizing extractive rent-realizing industries along with infrastructural industries would also have the advantage of producing tradable shares with which to generate capital markets. Moreover, they would be acceptable vehicles for organized international aid and investment institutions that are obligated to make a substantial portion of their financing to private firms. All in all, such industries present an ideal set of financeable and potentially privatizable activities, protected from the vicissitudes of markets and competition. They are not, however, very likely to be particularly generative of a new capitalist culture.

Those who expect a major capital injection from the West are likely to be disappointed. A "Marshall Plan" for the former Soviet empire is not in the cards. There will be dramatic differences among the host nations in the role of foreign capital. Foreign capital and foreign markets will be major shapers of the Czech economy; they will necessarily have only a small impact on the Russian economy.

Risky business conditions. Marko Simonetti, director of privatization for Slovenia, argues that the challenge of privatization is to find active owners willing to lead companies through the transition period. But why should new owners restructure their enterprises when there may be an immediate payoff if they simply liquidate the assets? Domestic producers will not be able to compete effectively in open markets, at home or through exports. A quick taste of what lies ahead is the case of large state enterprises in eastern Germany. Unable to compete abroad, these firms lost their home market when products and companies from the western part of the country moved in. The temptation to liquidate rather than to invest is heightened by the asset value of many companies. Expect rent-seeking, not entrepreneurship.

Weak links between labor, suppliers, manufacturers, and consumers. First World countries like Japan and Germany were able to get back on their feet quickly after World War II partly because reconstruction meant the reconstitution of forms of economic organization established years earlier rather than the creation of completely new relationships. For instance, keiretsu, the centralized forms of ownership in Japan, were antedated by *zaibatsu,* which originated in the Meiji era. German business and unions reached durable working arrangements long before the postwar German miracle. Eastern Europe will not be able to manufacture those relationships overnight.

Industrial structures did not develop according to economic logic; they were defined by planned linkages within the regions of the ex-Soviet empire. Isolated from world markets, large firms produced goods made better and more cheaply abroad. They operated in captive markets and exported on a large scale to similarly noncompetitive markets. They learned to operate with constant output and input prices and virtually unlimited access to credit. As one big firm in the region tries to improve itself by sourcing quality components from the world market, it dries up the markets for the other large firms, its traditional suppliers. When local consumers get a little real money and the choice to buy coveted imported goods rather than generally lower quality local product, the entire system collapses. Private investment—obtained in a real capital market—will not be readily forthcoming in newly privatized companies that are unsure of where their markets lie, where their sources of supply are located, or who their competitors are.

These obstacles would deter the most ardent reformers from attempting a program of drastic and potentially all-or-nothing industrial change. But the radical capitalists argue that it is essential to privatize quickly precisely because of such problems. That prescription might be tenable given a stable institutional setting with stable national boundaries and political systems, functioning tax codes, financial and legal systems, and broad-based capital markets, as well as plausibly operating networks of international markets and industrial linkages. But there are few credible tested institutions. Without them, rapid privatization will not provide a solid base for prosperity, nor will it aid the development of independent entrepreneurs.

THE CRUCIAL ROLE OF CAPITAL MARKETS

Capital markets, just one of the absent institutions, invite particular attention. Price-driven capital markets are dear to the hearts of privatizers. Capital markets remove power, in giant dollops, from the hands of entrenched bureaucracies. They are fast and powerful and provide invisibility for the market movers.

In capitalist economies, broad-based equity markets serve both investors and corporations alike in several ways. First, equity markets signal the underlying value of securities. Theoretically, this facilitates the proper allocation of resources by providing both investors and companies opportunities to raise cash as well as to spread resources among businesses which vary by product line and investment risk. Accurate share valuations also provide stockholders with a de facto evaluation of management, which may sometimes precipitate corrective action. Second, equity markets provide avenues for companies to raise capital (equity or debt) over a wide net of investors. By the same token, equity markets enable investors to control risk in their portfolio more easily. Finally, equity markets ease the costs of investment and corporate restructuring by providing liquidity to both investors and corporations alike.

Because they are so powerful, capital markets are dangerous, especially when they lack proper safeguards and depth. In the lands of the ex–Soviet empire, the hazards are particularly acute because of the complete lack of experience in using these markets. Additionally, capital markets are likely to attract more attention than usual because of their novelty in the region and their significance as a capitalist symbol. Radical capitalists assume, correctly in our view, that capital markets will arise concurrently with privatization and the issuance of shares. Despite few viable companies, public stock markets are being organized in most of the countries.

Unfortunately, in spite of good intentions, these equity markets probably will not be able to perform efficiently—and just may perform with delegitimating perversity. It will be virtually impossible to establish fair market value for the exchange's listed companies given the shortage of capital in the region and the unstable business conditions. The lack of well-established, highly capitalized market participants implies that there will be a lack of liquidity in the equity markets. This will produce thin equity markets and wild price swings.

Corruption is sure to become a big problem. Inexperienced market regulators will not be able to police markets that are moving quickly and without apparent reason. Market rigging and stock manipulation are inevitable. As most experienced traders will attest, financial market operations are very complex and enforcing fair rules can be nearly impossible. The first rounds of stock market activity are sure to see managers and their invisible partners in the administration cash in big. A crop of instant millionaires—whom everyone knew as the old nomenklatura—will become conspicuous symbols to be manipulated by potential demagogues.

If the resentment against black marketeers in Russia is any indication, there will be a groundswell against the "excessive" greed and corruption in the equity markets. Legitimate operators could get caught up in the popular outrage; so might the whole reform movement, especially in the context of large-scale economic misery and uncertainty experienced "by honest, hard working, native people."

PUBLIC ENTERPRISES RECONSIDERED

Radical capitalists insist that state ownership and capitalism do not mix, nor do state ownership and rapid development. In their view, the Communist economic malaise is just another failure of state ownership. Throughout the world, and in the Third World in particular, they argue, stated-owned industries are notoriously inefficient and corrupt. Little wonder that many poor nations, as diverse as India, Turkey, and Mexico, have embarked, quite successfully, on massive privatization programs in recent years.

Yet, state ownership makes sense at certain times, under certain conditions. For instance, when markets are quite imperfect and capital scarce, institutional malfunctions may channel investment away from those industries that are key to long-term development. In several countries, a sudden implosion of whole sectors, sometimes whole sets of sectors, has resulted in the state's finding itself forced to step in and nationalize the losers. Hence the typical state sector, with its portfolio of coal mines, steel mills, railways, and shipbuilding docks. Italy and Spain have lavish government portfolios so acquired. This history of nationalizing dying industries in response to political pressures or more simply of managing the difficult task of restructuring and downsizing as painlessly as possible has given state-owned enterprises their bad name. They are, most often, collections of basket cases that no one else would take. This is what makes their experience particularly relevant to big business in the former Communist realm.

There are, however, other examples of state-owned companies, nationalized for one reason or another, that were not already dying. France provides the best examples, and the history has been anything but negative. As late as thirty years after World War II, the French state still owned all or major firms in steel, coal, oil distribution, refining, transportation, automobiles, cigarettes, electronics, ocean shipping, aircraft, skyscraper office development, radio and television broadcasting, telephone services, gas, electricity, plus, horrid as it may seem, most big banks and insurance companies. And this is but a partial list. The postwar modernization, restructuring, and growth of the French economy has been, by anyone's standards (except Japan's), extraordinarily successful. What is more, state-owned firms played a leading role, not simply a shock-absorbing role, in that transformation and modernization.

In Japan and Korea the giant industrial groupings that dominate the economy defy simple classification as private or public. Nor is there any compelling reason to make the distinction. Surely the great Japanese keiretsu are not public firms; the government does not own them. But it is extremely difficult to assimilate the Sumitomo or Mitsubishi groups into the traditional category of a private firm. The market is not the opposite of the government; the firm is not in opposition to the state. There are many varieties of institutional arrangements, and they change with time and circumstance. The all-or-nothing, public bureaucracy or private (capital-market-based) firm is dangerously simplistic—especially as a guide for Russia, where capitalism does not yet exist. It pops out of textbook economics, not out of the history of successful economic development, especially "catch-up" development. That is the relevant genre: Russia does not have to invent its positive future—just catch up with it.

What determines the success of state-owned enterprises? State-operated industries can be operated efficiently or inefficiently, using technologically advanced production techniques or backward ones. Empirically, the answer is clear. Good performance is a function of the domestic political economy and its institutions, not just the fact of state ownership. Drawing from a cross-national collection of case studies of privatization, Raymond Vernon in *The Promise of Privatization* concluded:

> Where governments have been reasonably competent and responsible, and where comparisons between private enterprises and state-owned enterprises have been possible, the technical performance of state-owned enterprises has not appeared much different from that of private enterprises. Here and there a strikingly efficient performance by a state-owned enterprise has cast doubt on the simple stereotypes of the public enterprise as a perennial wastrel.[20]

In certain circumstances, reliance on the public sector and public ownership, in particular, may actually be good strategy. State ownership is certainly not to be sought as an end in itself, nor, for that matter, is private ownership of large enterprises. It all depends on the context in which choices must be made. Where private ownership seems doomed to fail—as in the case of many large enterprises in the ex–Soviet empire— the failure will result in a sudden implosion of the economy and society. In these cases, alternatives to simple privatization should be sought.

Furthermore, the recent surge of privatizations throughout Europe, Japan, and the Third World indicates that state ownership need not be permanent. Those trying to design new systems might profitably sift the rich varieties of institutional experience of other countries to see what made for better or worse performance: from state-owned, state-regulated, state-controlled, or state-in-cahoots-with. Ownership is a complex concept, contingent on embedded institutions. Given current conditions for big industry in the former Communist realms, some state ownership may be more desirable than simple "private ownership." Indeed, the logic of privatization in those lands does not ensure a dynamic market economy dominated by private firms. More likely, rapid privatization will precipitate state reintervention sooner or later.

THE FAULTY INSTITUTIONAL LOGIC OF RAPID PRIVATIZATION

The focus on privatization, and especially on rapid privatization, diverts attention from the implementation of policies and the creation of market firms and institutions that encourage the development of competitive industries and an effective state bureaucracy to ensure viable democratic societies.

More than increasing efficiency expected from privatization, these troubled nations need the benefit of rebuilding the networks of industrial linkages and trade within the region. They need outlets for goods—such as steel, ships, coal, and, especially, agriculture—to Western Europe; these will not be easy to obtain. They will need import controls so all savings will not wash out quickly in a wave of consumer buying. More than anything, they need competent and honest public administration to recreate those international linkages, administer those controls, negotiate those trade agreements, regulate the new and wildly imperfect markets, and buffer the shocks of industrial restructuring.

To the radical capitalists, rapid privatization is a shortcut. Eliminate the state, and voilà, economic growth. But this is myth, ideology. The state will not whither away, despite the dreams of the radical capitalists any more than it did in the dreams of Karl Marx. The state will run things for a long time, if not as owner, then as regulator.

Ironically, the logic of rapid privatization does not make the dependence of industry on the state any less likely. The state is destined to be the key economic player for the foreseeable future, whether privatization be rapid or gradual. Newly privatized giant enterprises will depend on the state for financing and for establishing rules and regulations. The state will also maintain a heavy hand in the industrial core of the economy because the inherited industrial structure provides most industries with too few firms for successful self-regulation by competition. And regulation by foreign competition may prove fatal.

Just as the state will necessarily be interventionist, given rapid privatization, so it will be protectionist. Assisted by their new armies of shareholders, the newly privatized enterprises, unfit to meet foreign competition, are likely to press for protectionist measures, especially since competing in an open economy would be suicidal. Free competition would open the field for Japan, the newly industrialized countries, and other low-cost, high-quality producers and leave little chance for inefficient domestic producers. They are inefficient now, and by world standards, they will be inefficient and uncompetitive for the near term. One must recall that Japan, Korea, France, and Germany never exposed their "infant industries" to the rigors of foreign competition.

Grand designs are associated with great risk. So it was with communism, so it will be with capitalism. The radical capitalists' fallacy is that pragmatism will ultimately result in the loss of discipline as local interests forestall change. Their concern is valid, but their prescription is not. The risks associated with rapid privatization skew the odds toward failure and ultimately toward disenchantment with capitalism and a democratic, more liberal state.

The big, inefficient enterprises will not succeed as private enterprises. But they cannot simply be abolished. Building the structures of capitalism, the institutions of a functioning market system, will take time and breathing room. Radically pure markets will not build them; they will destroy those structures and risk ending the capitalist experiment before it has had a chance to develop into something worthwhile. After all, it was Joseph Schumpeter, the great advocate of entrepreneurial capitalism, in his brilliant case for maintaining less than perfect markets, who remarked: "You put brakes on a car so that it can go faster, not slower."

IV

The contributors to this volume trace the disastrous consequences of Russia's radical capitalist reforms with a focus on the Russian institutional context. Their conclusions support the view that Russia's misery is quite understandable in retrospect and, therefore, foreseeable if not in degree, at least in both direction and cause.

Steven Fish, in his contribution provides an approach for understanding what he terms Russia's "racket economy"; he explains his use of that provocative term and, more important, why that situation came about. In addition to the critical vacuum in the realms of public morality and public associations—the inheritance of Soviet totalitarianism—he attributes key roles to a combination of three factors: 1) An economy rich in natural resources, gas, oil, metals, etc., that defined "rent-seeking" and not industrial development as the principal economic activity and route to capitalist profit; 2) The unfortunate way privatization was carried out: a hurried first phase that sprayed ownership vouchers about and created "nomenklatura privatization," and an even less fortunate second phase of "loans for shares" that fortified the private "banks"—the oligarchy that holds Russian economic assets and that now runs the economy and "runs Russian politics"; 3) The withdrawal of the state from the business of law enforcement.

Fish bravely explores possible routes out of the tunnel. Before economic and social reforms can be addressed, the Russian state must reestablish a monopoly over the use of force. This will require siphoning public resources from other key activities, including infrastructure development and social welfare programs. Fish further argues that the public sector needs to lead a drive to bolster potentially competitive high-value-added manufactures such as aircraft, automobiles, military hardware, and computers. Although he favors extending assistance to the institutions of civil society, including small business associations, academics, and intellectuals, it is only a newly invigorated state, in Fish's estimation, that can steer Russia out of its current dilemma.

This volume's other authors organize their contributions around the notion of "networks," the focus of the BRIE/Kreisky Forum project on "Unifying the European Economy." But these are not the "good" networks whose emergence forms the subject of *Enlarging Europe: The Industrial Foundations of a New Political Reality*, on the transition in Central and Eastern Europe. Russia's networks are barriers to economic development; they seek to suck out the assets of the state and to expand influence by extending tentacles throughout the Russian political and economic system. Partnership with strategic foreign partners is not a prime objective and, at times, can be unwelcome.

Gregory Grossman begins before privatization, before perestroika and glasnost, and explains how a hidden economy, growing rapidly during the terminal decades of the Soviet order, culminated in the subordination of the formal apparatus of governance and truly came into dominance in the newly privatized Russia. Aside from the corruption of state and party, which fostered the widespread creation of illicit private income and wealth, he cites the aggravations of regional, sectoral, and ethnic tensions and the related rise of organized crime as factors in the emergence of the hidden economy. Although the underground sector may have stimulated enterprise and inculcated mutual trust, it reinforced the tendency to loot the state, dodge taxes, and cheat customers. Grossman's revealing study of the penetration of organized crime in every sector and niche of the Soviet economy and administration provides a key for understanding not only the decline of the old order, but also the challenges faced by the democratic structures that have sought to replace it.

In their study of Russian business networks, Peter Huber and Andreas Wörgötter analyze the unequal competition between "survivalist" and "entrepreneurial" networks in the new Russia. Survivalist networks, which grew rapidly during the final decades of state socialism, currently dominate the post-Soviet political economy. Born in conditions engendering conspiratorial methods and based on personal ties rather than impersonal commercial relations, they focus on reinforcing their power to extract rents rather than the ability to compete in open markets. In many cases, such networks are based on large enterprises that dominate entire regions, including local administrative structures, which gives them the ability to counter worker demands and wall out potential competitors. Needless to say, while the members of survivalist networks have welcomed FDI, their goals often diverge fundamentally from those of their Western partners. Huber and Wörgötter also chart the emergence of entrepreneurial networks, which tend to form in regions lacking a single hegemonic firm and in sectors that are less concentrated. Although more sanguine observers have suggested that survivalist networks can be expected to decline as they kill off the hosts on which they feed, Huber and Wörgötter argue that survivalist networks could hold on for the foreseeable future, contributing to the isolation of Russia's business networks and the country's relative isolation.

Manuel Castells's analysis of the development of a third form of Russian business networks, predatory networks, draws out the implications of Russia's misdevelopment for the country's future role in the European and global economies. Although the new Russia inherited an enormous economic potential, it exercises a mere shadow of its potential influence because of the collapse of sophisticated manufacturing in the post-Soviet years. Castells attributes Russia's abrupt and unprecedented deindustrialization to the decline of the Soviet military-industrial complex, the dismantling of the centrally planned economy before the emergence of functioning markets, and the impoverishment of the Russian population, the last a consequence of ill-advised macroeconomic adjustment programs. The paradoxical result of Russia's particularly abrupt privatization has been an increased dependence on exports of fuel and energy to pay for needed imports of food and producer goods—along with luxury consumer goods for the new rich. One of the most harmful trends has been the disruption of Russia's high technology industries, including the electronics sector, which may end up as a low-level subsidiary to third-tier Asian producers. Castells rejects the idea that foreign investment will solve Russia's difficulties. More important, the primary form of integration of the Russian economy in the international financial circuits results from the recycling of profits from the shadow economy.

The networks that have grown up in Russia are not instruments of development. Their international extensions are a growing problem for many countries. In a moment where enthusiasm for a globalizing economy led by private investment and private actors is perhaps excessive, they remind us of the critical role played by national institutions, especially the key institution of an effective, responsible public administration.

NOTES

1. This chapter extends an earlier essay, Stephen S. Cohen and Andrew Schwartz, "The Tunnel at the End of the Light," which was published as BRIE Working Paper No. 56 (September 1992); in *American Prospect*, no. 13 (Spring 1993); and, in Russian, in *EKO*, vol. 9, no. 231, and vol. 10, no. 232 (1993).
2. See the chapter by Manuel Castells in this volume.
3. Marshall I. Goldman, "Russia's Reform Effort: Is There Growth at the End of the Tunnel?," *Current History*, October 1997, p. 313. For a very different view that seeks rather heroically to show a less dismal economic performance, see Simon Johnson, Daniel Kaufmann, and Andrei Shleifer, "The Unofficial Economy in Transition," *Brookings Papers on Economic Activity*, no. 2 (1997). Shleifer, a Harvard professor, has been an actor in Russia's privatization through the Harvard Institute of International Development—not without controversy. He has written extensively, and generally in very positive terms, about the effects of Russian privatization. In this piece, econometric models are developed on the basis of estimates of the post-privatization (but not the pre-privatization) "black economy" to generate higher indicators of actual economic activity. In this same vein, see also Maxim Boycko, Andrei Shleifer, and Robert W. Vishy, *Privatizing Russia* (Cambridge: MIT Press, 1995).
4. Michael Hout and Theodore P. Gerber, "More Shock than Therapy," *American Journal of Sociology*, July 1998.
5. Marshall I. Goldman, "Comments and Discussion," in *Brookings Papers on Economic Activity*, no. 2 (1997), p. 229.
6. Castells in this volume.
7. World Bank, unpublished data, and UNCTAD, *World Investment Report*, 1996, annex tables 1 and 5. Even if we subtract about 25 percent to serve as an estimate for "round tripping"—that is, funds that originate in China, leave the country (usually to Hong Kong), and then return nicely laundered as "foreign investment"—the magnitudes depict another reality from that of Russia.
8. See Peter Nolan, *China's Rise, Russia's Fall* (New York: St. Martin's Press, 1995), p. 16, tables 2.4 and 2.5.
9. See *ibid.*, p. 19.
10. *Ibid.*, p. 20; see also M. Ellman, "The Increase in Death and Disease under Katastroika," *Cambridge Journal of Economics* 18, 4: 329–56.
11. Cohen and Schwartz, "The Tunnel."
12. For a full discussion, see Andrew Schwartz, "The Best Laid Plan: The Unanticipated Evolution of Privatization in the Czech Republic"; Ph.D. dissertation, University of California at Berkeley, forthcoming.

13. Graham Allison and Grigory Yavlinsky, "Window of Opportunity: Joint Program for Western Cooperation in the Soviet Transformation to Democracy and the Market Economy" (Cambridge, Mass.: Harvard University, 1991); mimeo, pp. 3–4.
14. Ronald H. Coase, "The Problem of Social Cost," *Journal of Law and Economics* 3 (1960): 1–44.
15. Boycko et al.
16. The policy recommendation of the Institute of EastWest Studies is typical: "If concessions to managers and workers must be given in order to move privatization ahead, policy-makers should ensure that: . . . *workers get as little as possible*" (Institute for EastWest Studies, "Policy Recommendations on Banks, Capital Markets, and Enterprise Restructuring"; sponsored by EBRD, World Bank, UN Development Program, 1994), p. 20.
17. See Cohen and Schwartz, "The Tunnel."
18. Jeffrey Sachs, "Accelerating Privatization in Eastern Europe: The Case of Poland"; World Bank Annual Conference on Development Economics, 25 and 26 April 1991, p. 1.
19. "Survey of Business in Eastern Europe," *The Economist*, 21 September 1991, p. 5.
20. Raymond Vernon, *The Promise of Privatization: A Challenge for U.S. Policy* (New York: Council on Foreign Relations, 1988).

SUBVERTED SOVEREIGNTY: HISTORIC ROLE OF THE SOVIET UNDERGROUND

Gregory Grossman

> The greatest intellectual challenge raised by the fall of the Soviet empire is not to construct a theory or praxis of transition to capitalism, but to explain why and how, for the first time in history, a great empire and a great civilization collapsed in a few years without the glory of a military disaster or the tragedy of a civil war.
>
> – Seurot 1996 (opening lines)

> If . . . anything is ever to occur to disrupt the unity and efficacy of the Party as a political instrument, Soviet Russia might be changed overnight from one of the strongest to one of the weakest and most pitiable of national societies.
>
> – "Mr. X" [Kennan] (1947: 572)

In a partial and modest way the present paper addresses François Seurot's challenge by proposing a thesis that the USSR's shadow economy and the rest of its underground—misappropriation, corruption, organized crime—in the end contributed to the system's collapse.[1] The main elements in this demolition process were the following:

(i) The rapid and unbounded rise of the shadow economy, especially in the terminal decades of the USSR;

(ii) Widespread and at times very large illicit wealth in private hands; and

(iii) The attendant ubiquitous and all-permeating corruption of management and officialdom of every stripe and rank, followed by

(iv) An explosion of violent organized crime (linked to (i)–(iii) above;

(v) The simultaneous growth of informal horizontal (managerial, bureaucratic, political) networks within the official hierarchical pyramid, strengthening horizontal ties at some expense of the formal vertical ones;

(vi) A concurrent aggravation of inter-regional and inter-ethnic economic inequalities accentuated the centrifugal tendencies within the Soviet society.

In sum, this covert process culminated in subordination of much of the formal apparatus of rule and control within the party-state hierarchy and in the severance or fraying of vertical lines of communication and authority, as it reoriented the nomenklatura's private (or group) interests and loyalties toward the new, nonofficial sources of wealth and power—with dire consequences for empire, union, system, and economy. We lay no claim that this argument provides the chief, let alone the sole, explanation of the Great Collapse. Certainly, a fuller understanding must invoke countless other causal factors and processes—if not One Big Cause.

As for Seurot's query, in what manner indeed could, "for the first time in history, a great empire and a great civilization [collapse] in a few years without a military disaster or . . . a civil war"? In the crucial months of August–December 1991, the smoke of defeat in Afghanistan was still lingering in the air, but it was hardly the "glorious" defeat implied in the epigraph. No Union-wide civil war either, but popular frustration there was aplenty—with the economy, Afghanistan, and much more. True, several serious but local cases of overt popular activism occurred from 1988 on—in Armenia and in the Baltic republics—and some major strikes in the Slavic republics beginning in the summer of 1989. Serious as these were, for the USSR as a whole, the definitive moves took place at the levels of high nomenklatura and political leadership. The endgame was played out primarily by clashing personalities, ambitions, and interests. In the end, a farce of a coup (August 1991), followed by a successful countercoup, brought down an edifice of power and statehood that had already been badly corroded.

How had that edifice been so compromised? Much has already been written on this topic, and many fingers have pointed at the Soviet economy. And yet, a close and keen observer could still underscore in mid-1997 that a significant puzzle persists: why did the enormous Soviet nomenklatura, armed to the teeth with loyal internal forces, fail to defend either socialism or the Union with all its might? . . . Something needs to be explained (Kotkin 1997: 104).

In the ongoing lively discussion of the etiology of the Great Collapse, *economic* causes (or intermediate causes, sources, factors) have received wide attention. To mention a few that are widely cited in this context:[2]

- The long-term decline in rates of overall economic growth, from high ones in the 1950s and 1960s down to around zero;
- A protracted and extremely burdensome arms race, combined with hyper-militarization of the economy;
- High costs of empire and of global reach;
- Serious lags in technology, particularly in electronics;
- Sticky long-term problems in agriculture, leading to dependence on imported food and fodder and to heavy and growing burdens on the treasury and the balance of payments;
- Unhelpful demographic trends;
- As already mentioned, a rapidly growing shadow economy (which may have had its positive effects as well, and, in any case, its rapid growth somewhat compensates for the steady retardation of the official economy);
- Fiscal woes and mounting repressed/hidden/open inflation;
- A severe and swelling environmental crisis;
- Toward the end, exhaustion or depletion of most of the Soviet economy's readily usable material and financial, not to say moral, reserves;
- Moreover, in the USSR (as in other "socialist" countries), a succession of inept, partial, repeatedly failing economic reforms eroded confidence in the future of the traditional system, accelerating the fall as it began to sway.

But the Soviet Union's terminal decades were not without major *positive* economic developments as well. Two of them occupy pride of historical place: the steep rise in petroleum extraction between 1960 and 1980—about fourfold for oil, about tenfold for natural gas—and the sudden and continued rise in world energy prices—about twelvefold (for oil) from 1972 to the early 1980s. Their combined effect constituted a gigantic windfall, especially for an economy already in a long-term downslide.[3] Among other things, thanks to the sharp improvement in the USSR's terms of trade with the West, it boosted hard-currency earnings and consequently also the national budget revenue (in domestic rubles) from external economic activity (thus holding down inflation); ensured *valuta* cover for the growing food and fodder imports, and hence the maintenance of basic consumption levels; and permitted the continuance of the huge military program.

In this manner, the petroleum windfall favored the then conservative regime, perhaps even prolonged its life by putting off a Gorbachevian perestroika by some years. Conceivably—only conceivably—it might have even provided an economic springboard and reserve for a decisive institutional transformation of the economy and the system—which did not happen, of course. The regime was neither able nor willing to turn the windfall of the 1960s and 1970s to any such end (Brezhnev lasted till November 1982); and, as history shows, it was also unable to utilize the windfall to brake the long-term retardation and deterioration of economic performance within the traditional framework.

By the mid-1980s the opportunities vanished. Soviet oil and gas output peaked. World energy prices crashed. The arms race escalated. Gorbachev, perestroika, and glasnost were waiting in the wings, as it were. A more fateful future lurked beyond them.

1986 AND ALL THAT

Gorbachev stepped in as general-secretary of the Communist Party (CP) of the Soviet Union in March 1985. Although perestroika and glasnost doubtless helped pave the way toward the Great Collapse—some students pin most of the responsibility on them—here we limit our account to only a few facets of that now well-known story.

Gorbachev's institutional economic reforms began in the second half of the following year with modest but pathmaking measures. Three of them deserve mention, being noteworthy reform-wise, and soon to become notorious collapse-wise as well: (1) a very limited devolution of authority for foreign economic relations to state-owned firms (August 1986); (2) minor expansion in the scope of legal, small-scale ("individual") private activity (November); and (3) in the short run the most important of the three, legalization of a new type of producers' cooperative, initiated from below, socialist in name, private in content (October). Reasonable enough for the start of a partial (not system-transforming) economic reform, but. . . . In just a few years, (1) turned into a cornucopia from which just-privatized capital gushed abroad by the billions of U.S. dollars; (2) did more to shelter further expansion of illicit private ("shadow") activity than to promote lawful small-scale activity;[4] and (3) was turned into a captive legal entity for asset- and profit-stripping in the state sector on a vast scale.

A recent article by Solnick (1996) presents an apposite, incisive analysis of the weakening of the formal Soviet economic hierarchy during perestroika. Proceeding from a "neoinstitutionalist perspective" and employing a conceptual and analytical structure resting on an organization-theoretic and game-theoretic foundation as applied to large formal heirarchies and their internal principal-agent relations, the author sets out to explain the reasons for the strikingly different outcomes of the Soviet and Chinese reforms of the 1980s.

Here we bypass his discussion of the Chinese reform and of the contrast with the Soviet one. In regard to perestroika, Solnick offers three case studies. The first is the devolution of managerial powers from the ministries and other high-level bodies in the Soviet economic-administrative hierarchy down to the enterprises, particularly as exemplified by the 1987 Law on State Enterprises. A crucial factor is the unclarity of the distribution of property rights between hierarchical levels (and of course also the lack of workable market policy variables). The author shows how this quickly led to loss of information and control by the "principals" and opportunism—including spontaneous de facto privatization—by the "agents," at times in collusion with state bureaucrats. He stresses the snowball-like dynamics of the process (what he calls a "bank run"). Solnick's other two cases are descriptively somewhat different but theoretically similar to the first in conditions and outcome—namely, federal-republican relations from 1989 on and the CP. (Rather, because of the paucity of materials on the CP itself and relative abundance on the Young Communist League, the author uses the latter as proxy for the former.)

Solnick's findings, primarily in his first (economic) case, are consistent with the hypothesis put forth above regarding the formal apparatus of rule and control, the severance or fraying of vertical lines of communication, the reorientation of the nomenklatura's interests and loyalties, etc.—with two major differences: in our scheme the shadow economy and the underground play crucial roles, while Solnick touches on them only obliquely, and in our scheme the process of hierarchical dissolution begins much earlier, though it gathers scope and force in the later years of the USSR.

We now turn to the underground.

THE SHADOW ECONOMY

Our object of study—proscribed (tabooed?) economic activity, tax evasion, black markets, etc.—is at least as old as history, perhaps exceeded in venerability only by the oldest profession. But its intense study on a global scale is very new. As if in a common response to the *Zeitgeist*, spontaneously and mostly unrelatedly, serious research on the "other" economies (informal, underground), of one's own and other countries, sprang up by the dozen in the decade from the mid-1970s to the mid-1980s (as can be confirmed by consulting the extensive bibliography in Dallago 1990).

In the USSR, centralized research on the overall shadow economy apparently began in the middle or later 1970s—needless to say, in official institutions and strictly behind closed doors. There seems to have been no professional collective term for this set of illegal or "semi-legal" economic activities until about that time, when the phrase "shadow economy" (*tenevaia ekonomika*) made its appearance, first among specialists and only years later (under glasnost) in public print as well.

In 1976, in the hope of at least partly filling a lacuna in Western understanding of Soviet reality, in both the quantitative and institutional senses, Professor Vladimir G. Treml (Duke University) and the present author launched the Berkeley-Duke Project on the Second Economy in the USSR. Only much later did we become aware of the just-mentioned Soviet studies. The Project focused on that realm of Soviet economic activity (and the corresponding personal/private income and wealth) which, legally or illegally, escaped or lay outside the official structure of planning, administration, and control. To denote it we chose the term "second economy" and formulated it as the aggregate of economic activities which satisfy at least one of the two following criteria: (1) being directly on private account, whether conducted legally or illegally; (b) being (to the actor) knowingly illegal in some substantial respect(s), done on either private or socialist account.[5] Needless to say, in the classical Soviet case both tests were typically met at once. (The risk of breaking the law on *socialist* account tended to be conditioned on the prospect of somebody's *personal* reward.) Illegal activities and the incomes therefrom would, naturally, not be reported (or not as such), and a considerable part of those legal in principle (e.g., private work by licensed "individual" tradesmen or professionals) would also not be reported to evade taxation or other risks.

"*Shadow* economy," on the other hand, was the preferred term in the USSR itself, and remains such in post-Soviet Russia. While it seems to be rarely rigorously defined, generally it omits *legal* private activities and in this respect at least is narrower than "second economy" in our sense.[6] In the present paper we employ either term, as befits the context, and use "underground" to refer to the totality of criminal activity, whether economic or not.

A final caveat: Whether "shadow" or "second," whether open or hidden, the "other" economy is not to be thought of as distinct and separate from the official economy. The two have been not a pair but a duality, symbiotic, often both mutually parasitic and mutually protective, always highly interdependent.

During most of the Communist era and (for the present purpose) particularly from about 1929 to about 1988, Soviet law severely constrained and heavily taxed lawful gainful activity on private account. Indeed, even when legal, it was officially termed "personal" or "individual" rather than private, for ideological reasons. Thus, for some sixty years legal private/personal activity *as such* was of very little economic consequence except for a few noteworthy instances ("personal subsidiary agriculture," home ownership). More often than not, it served as a screen for the much more lucrative and important illegal private pursuits.

Laws against so-called economic crime were far from fully enforced in the USSR. A case in point is the illegal direct dealing—usually barter—between state-owned firms. Generally, such deals were done with relative impunity though with circumspection. Part of the smaller-scale illegal economic doings by and between private individuals was also essentially ignored by the law—e.g., much of the ubiquitous stealing on the job or the provision of widespread personal services such as private tutoring and room painting. (A former officer in the Soviet economic police in the 1970s said in a Project interview that he would not be bothered with cases where individuals only doubled their legitimate income by operating "on the left"—i.e., illegally or informally.) Moreover, major infractions were often deliberately not recorded and suppressed but left to be exploited for personal gain (through extortion, blackmail) by law-enforcement and other state or Party officials. Not uncommonly, initiative for new "shadow" activities came from official authorities themselves.

THE LENGTHENING SHADOW

By 1960 the Soviet shadow economy was already institutionally mature and of notable scope and size. In the early 1960s it was the target of a fierce campaign by Khrushchev to the point of reintroduction of the death penalty.[7] In the event, this campaign, like all others against "economic crime" before and since, did little to set back the steady, rapid rise of illicit activity. Instead, the shadow economy spread out, grew, and prospered—under Brezhnev (1964–82), thanks to benign neglect if not tacit encouragement; under Gorbachev, in part owing to all the moving, shaking, and laxing of perestroika, as already noted. And so during the last three decades of the Soviet era, illegal economic activity penetrated into every sector and chink of the economy; assumed every conceivable shape and form; and operated on a scale ranging from the minimal or modest for the masses to the substantial for many, to the lavish and gigantic, as well as elaborately organized, for some.[8]

An extreme but not necessarily unique case of elaborate organization is the cotton fraud. For several years running in the 1970s and 1980s, the nominal size of the domestic cotton crop was boldly and deftly padded to rake in billions of rubles. Thousands were bought off in the process, including Brezhnev's son-in-law. Characteristically, the scam's chief perpetrators and beneficiaries were none other than the top Party and government leaders of Uzbekistan and other southern cotton-growing republics and—it has been alleged but never formally proven—a very high-level clique in the Kremlin.[9]

Much has been written on the virtues and faults of the shadow (or second) economy in the USSR and other Communist countries.[10] Where the official economy failed, the shadow economy provided, in quantity and/or quality, many goods and services for the public's everyday needs and comforts, while furnishing the income to afford them. It catered to demand ignored by the planners, such as that stemming from youth culture, religious and customary observances, artistic preferences, the quest for luxuries by the moneyed, and from the tastes and pursuits of sociocultural and dissident minorities. Most important, the shadow economy led to private accumulation and concentration of private wealth, while providing the material goods or foreign valuta for storing it, the domestic currency and official savings deposits being undependable. In some respects, it reopened Peter's window to the West. It stimulated enterprise, ingenuity, self-reliance, and saving, as well as general familiarity with a private exchange economy, in advance of their time. It inculcated mutual trust into transactions where nothing could be committed to writing. But it also confirmed such practices as robbing the state, tax dodging, cheating the customer, and every form of corruption, as a natural and durable way of life.

On its own part, the state often benefited directly from the lubricating effect of the underground economy and indirectly in many other ways as well. But the shadow economy could be costly to the state and to society. Because the theft or abuse of state property was the chief source of material supply for the shadow economy, a ten-ruble private gain might entail a thousand-ruble property loss to the state, not to say a million-ruble risk of a building collapse, a railway disaster, or an industrial explosion. Last but not least, by comparison, much of the shadow economy relegated much of what was done officially and formally by the state (and collective farms) to inferior quality and status.

Under Soviet conditions, with a disequilibrated economy and a corrupted officialdom and public, there were untold ways of making big money and large private fortunes and many more ways to make some money or derive some benefit. The personal risk varied from near-zero for the smallest fry to very high for the bigger underground dealers (Russian, *del'tsy* [pl.]).

One arrangement, however, deserves special mention because of its importance and distinctiveness—namely, *the crypto-private technique.* By this we mean illegal production on private account conducted behind the protective facade of a state (or other socialist) entity. The article produced illegally on private account is entirely identical with the legitimate article, both being produced on the same premises, the same production line, of the same quality, and by the same equipment, workers, and materials. They are usually sold at the same official, fixed price. Thus, the illicit and the legitimate products are mutually indistinguishable by the ultimate buyer or by an inspector, an obvious advantage for the underground entrepreneur, who is usually an insider of the legitimate entity. The private profit—often very large—derives not from charging a black market price, but from the unauthorized diversion of state or "socialist" owned materials, labor, machine time, etc., mostly secured by bribery and corruption, as is also the overall protection of the whole operation.[11] (The crypto-private producers among the del'tsy are known as *tsekhoviki* [pl.].) Our Project's interviews uncovered instances of the crypto-private sort going back to at least the immediate post–World War II years. The technique may well be older than that. Once perfected, it spread rapidly.

Looser variants of virtual privatization of production facilities under the Soviets are, e.g., (a) "on the left" custom manufacture of furniture or garments in state-owned workshops for private gain, and (b) the long-standing, almost ubiquitous, illicit practice of transporting unauthorized goods in state-owned trucks for the drivers' personal gain, using the state's gasoline, etc. In the latter case, the truck is de facto virtually privatized, but with the initial investment borne by the state. Other means of transport, even maritime shipping (the present author knows of one actual case), were similarly quasi-privatized by the underground already in the Soviet period.

CORRUPTION

The ubiquity of corruption in the Soviet Union has already been adverted to. All but the tiniest illegal (or even legal) gainful activities entailed payoffs to actual or potential spoilers, extortionists, trouble-makers, informers, and, not last, law enforcers.[12] The payoffs might be in cash, in kind, in favors, or whatever. They might be periodic and regular (i.e., tribute) or ad hoc and variable. Some payments were to the next higher level in the formal hierarchy; others were lateral—to outside auditors and inspectors, law enforcement officials, suppliers and transporters, bankers, and last but not least, Party officials. However, most lateral bribe recipients were embedded in their own formal hierarchies or structures, and thus typically also had to share their receipts up-hierarchy and/or laterally.

Such partial retaining and passing on up of corrupt income occurred at each level of every hierarchy, *including* those of the Party, general government, and economic police (OBKhSS). One can picture the wealth flowing up-channel through the pyramid, swelling as it rises along what might be called "loot chains" (by analogy with food chains that concentrate nutrients or toxins).[13] And since the apexes of all formal Soviet pyramids ultimately converged at the superapex of the country's leadership, so did the private wealth. Thus, we read in the reminiscences of a keen inside observer that when officials of the Central Committee entered Chernenko's office following his death (on 7 March 1985), they found "desk drawers stuffed with banknotes. Banknotes also filled half of the General Secretary's personal secret office safe" (Grachev 1994: 92).

"R'S" STORY

For a factual example of this process we turn to one of the open-ended interviews of the Berkeley-Duke Project. (All names and some facts in this account are masked to preserve anonymity.) R was a mid-level business administrator in a local organization running several dozen retail stores in a large city in the European USSR. The time is the mid-1960s. Each store had to meet its official monthly sales plan (in rubles) and usually did; these results appeared on the books. In addition, each store was informally but compellingly required by the superior organization to rake in a large amount of "left (illegal) money" that was kept off the books and which, on the average, added some 40 percent (!) to the recorded receipts. Chief sources of the "left money" were via (a) cheating customers in terms of quantity and quality, (b) cheating the produce-delivering collective farms (by bribing the farms' representatives), and (c) obtaining supplies on the cheap from irregular sources, such as crypto-private operations (see above).

At the bottom of the loot chain, every sales clerk was expected to cheat customers. She kept a part of the proceeds—which might double or treble her formal salary—and surrendered the rest to the store manager. The latter in his turn kept a part of these and other "left" receipts. The manager paid bribes on the level of the store to various inspectors and authorities (including internal Party and trade union secretaries, store accountants, etc.); kept some of the "left money" for himself, which multiplied his official earnings severalfold; and passed on a hefty sum to the next higher level in the trade organization. The same process of retention, redistribution, and upward passing repeated itself at every successive level, with the absolute take swelling progressively. Party functionaries were, naturally, included at each level.

R fleshed out his story with much numerical information, which we bypass here. Regular periodic collection of "left money" from individual stores was in fact one of his duties. About once a month he would pay a business visit to the republic official in charge of trade. Upon being ushered into the office, R would lay a fat envelope with money on the official's desk before their meeting could begin. No doubt the official passed on yet fatter envelopes to those above him.

The general picture of such capillary flow of large amounts of money up the loot chain has been amply corroborated by other emigrants and by innumerable accounts or allusions in the Soviet (and later Russian) press. The value of R's account is not that it is unique, but in that it was laden with concrete (and prima facie reliable) figures, thanks to the opportunity of interaction between interviewer and informant. In R's opinion, this system of distribution of "left money" had existed, in his organization and elsewhere, for some time previously and had not changed much afterwards except for steady growth in the ruble volumes of both legal and illegal money flows.

SOME FIGURES

Furtive and hidden by its very nature, the shadow economy is difficult to observe and measure. In the Soviet (or Soviet-type) case, it further frustrates the student owing to an economy characterized by macro-disequilibrium, across-the-board administrative price control, and repressed inflation. Price control is at once a spawning ground of illegal activity and a cause of wide variation in price ratios between the legal and illegal sectors. How does the real content of one million rubles in the black market compare with that of one million rubles in the official sector? At the same time in the same place it may be much less (higher prices in the black market); it may be more (lower-than-official prices, which is not uncommon either).[14] Worse, what is the theoretical meaning of the official, controlled prices, anyway? In a word, all "shadow" values are indeed such in more senses than one.

This said, we cite the well-known (but little explained) figures of the growth of the Soviet shadow economy by T. I. Koriagina, a leading Soviet specialist on the subject. She found that from the early 1960s to the late 1980s the nominal value of "shadow" sales in the USSR rose eighteenfold, from 5 to 90 billion rubles per year.[15] Again, all such estimates are rough at best, but in addition, they may incorporate inputs from the official economy, as well as harbor internal double-counting. In other words, they are at best approximate gross values, not value-added-in-the-shadow-economy figures. Nevertheless, their dynamics may be compared with the dynamics of the nominal values of official (recorded) national income (net material product) and of state retail sales of goods and services, each of which increased four- or fivefold—as against eighteenfold—over the same span of 25–30 years. In 1988, official retail sales of goods and services amounted to 422 billion rubles—to which, at first pass, the 90 billion rubles of shadow sales add over 20 percent in nominal terms. (To repeat, in the USSR, prices in the shadow economy have usually [not always] been higher, often much higher, than the official fixed prices.)

Methodologically independent support of the hypothesis of rapid growth of the second economy during the last Soviet decades is provided by an ingenious econometric exercise. Treml and Alexeev examined

> the relationships between per capita legal money income and such income-dependent variables as purchases of various goods and services in state trade in a large number of regions in Russia and Ukraine . . . between 1965 and 1989. The relationships display, not unexpectedly, a high degree of correspondence between income and most dependent variables in the 1965–70 period. . . . [After] 1965, and virtually without exception the close degree of correlation . . . begins to get weaker . . . and almost disappears by the end of the 1980s.

The authors "speculate that the most likely explanation of this phenomenon is the emergence and rapid growth of the second economy" and its unequal regional development. They stress that the implications of the second economy for the entire economy are "not unequivocal" (in part because of the ambiguity of the relevant objective function—GG). They conclude:

> As long as the second economy operates on the margins, its effect seems to be mostly beneficial. . . . When [it] grows too large, however, its role seems to become more dysfunctional. . . . The growth of the second economy probably was . . . not the principal reason, for the disintegration of the Soviet economic system.[16]

Let us remember, however, that the authors' attention is on economic efficiency and overall economic performance. They are only incidentally concerned with the indirect effects of the second (or shadow) economy on the viability of the formal hierarchy of governance—and, hence, of the overall Soviet system—working through such channels as corruption, violent crimes, erosion of discipline, material differentiation, and the reorientation of loyalties.

The underground economy, a natural if illegitimate offspring of the Soviet system, accomplished with time what was not supposed to happen: a huge accumulation of private wealth and capital. The larger lumps of illicit wealth were located in two social foci: among the big shadow economy operators and among the higher state and Party nomenklatura on local, republican, and union levels. Smaller but still significant and surely numerous lumps of wealth were much more widely distributed.

The del'tsy and the nomenklatura needed one another. The former had ample money but required protection from law enforcement and sundry predators, as well as informal access to the state's resources. The authorities could provide both. On its part, the nomenklatura had power and connections but needed money, wealth. The last may seem puzzling. Was the nomenklatura not lavished by the regime with precious privileges and benefits, especially in the higher ranks of Party and government officialdom?[17] It was. But the regime granted these privileges not so much in money as in rare and "deficit" goods *in kind*, or by selling them at large discounts—a strategy that minimized the possibility to accumulate personal wealth and maximized the individual's dependence on the regime for the good life and, hence, his good behavior.[18]

But the nomenklatura was never secure in the regime's favors. A purge, disgrace, demotion, or death of the caviar-winner could throw the family far down the affluence scale, even into poverty, if not worse. On the other hand, personal material security for the future could come from independent (read: corrupt) accumulation of wealth—as it were, from Faustian deals with the underworld (though it is not always clear which was the Devil).[19] Such deals carried their own heavy risks, though less so after Brezhnev came to power.

Personal security was not the only motive of large accumulation of wealth by the mighty. At times it seems to have become its own end, or rather the means of establishing a veritable fiefdom in which the baronial lord would enjoy near absolute power, constrained only by "them" in Moscow (or in Tashkent, or Baku, or Alma Ata). While "they" had the final word, "they" could be bought off and flattered to leave one in secure possession of the fiefdom, so long as the same "they" stayed in power. Within this private domain, the first secretary of the Party held all the tools for absolute sway: administrative, coercive and violent, propaganda, and (not least) economic power (particularly in the shadow economy, with himself at the top of the loot chain). This condition perhaps obtained in most pronounced form primarily in the southern republics. But, in principle if in attenuated forms, it obtained also in northern localities (particularly in some provincial centers and rural areas). Anecdotal information and some serious but mostly nonquantitative studies invariably pointed to a much greater development of the shadow economy in the south (Transcaucasia and Central Asia) than in the north (the European USSR). One could therefore expect a similar disparity in terms of per-household or per-capita income and wealth.

The findings of the Berkeley-Duke Project tend to bear this out. Our fixed questionnaire survey has a total sample of 1,061 households, 3,023 persons. The south enters the sample in two ways: (i) A subsample of 191 households of ethnic Armenians who had emigrated from Armenia (as against those who had resided elsewhere in the Soviet Union) to the United States in the 1970s. At the time, besides indigenous Georgian and Central Asian Jews leaving for Israel, this Armenian emigration was the only mass emigration of persons of southern nationality from the Soviet south; (ii) Another but nonindigenous group of recent emigrants from the south consisted of ethnic "northerners" (mostly European Jews) whose last places of residence were in the south. From this group we collected a subsample 142 households. They had all resided in capital cities of southern republics and in this sense are a homogeneous group.

Our survey found that Armenians from Armenia indeed had a much greater pecuniary benefit from the second economy than did our households from the north (European USSR). Notably, Group (ii), our northerners from the south, display an economic profile somewhere between those of the north and of the Armenians.

The data in the text table (below) address personal income and personal wealth on a *per-capita annual mean basis* for these two southern subsamples, compared to subsamples from the north. They pertain to the end of the 1970s and to the urban population alone (then over 60 percent of the total Soviet population) and, for greater comparability, relate only to households in which both members of the main adult couple were present, of whom at least one was working in the "first" economy at the time. (We collected data from other types of households as well.)

LSI stands for legitimate income from socialist sources; it does not include the imputed value of free legal services from the socialist sector, such as education and health care, or of subsidies to consumer goods and services. AOI stands for all other income—that is, legal and illegal income from all private sources and illicit income from socialist sources (e.g., theft). LSI + AOI = total income per capita.

Column (4) shows for each region the weighted mean ratio of AOI to LSI; column (5), the weighted mean ratio of per capita personal wealth to LSI (the dimension of this column is, of course, years). Absolute values for wealth are not in the table but can be computed by multiplying column (5) by column (2).

Thus, in our sample, in regard to full working households: For Armenians from Armenia (AA), mean AOI was 2,065 rubles per year per person, close to double mean LSI. For the north, AOI was one-third as much, 657 rubles, and brought LSI up by only one-half. For the northerners from the south, AOI was equal to LSI. For AA, mean wealth was 13,745 rubles per person; for the north, it was 3,450 rubles—only one-fourth as much; for northerners from the south it was 5,895 rubles.

These figures are for the late 1970s. Circumstantial evidence suggests that a decade later the contrast between the north and the south was at least as great and probably substantially greater.

	Number of Persons (1)	LSI[a] (*Rubles per year*) (2)	AOI[b] (3)	AOI: LSI[c] (4)	Wealth: LSI[d] (*Years*) (5)
North (European USSR)	[1,609]	1,291	657	0.51	2.76
RSFSR and Baltics	[1,051]	1,287	541	0.42	2.80
Moscow	[166]	1,643	764	0.47	3.34
Leningrad	[294]	1,405	538	0.38	3.09
Ukraine, Belorussia, Moldavia	[558]	1,300	874	0.67	2.68
Armenians from Armenia	[560]	1,155	2,065	1.79	11.90
Northerners from south	[488]	896	887	0.99	6.58

[a] Legitimate income from socialist sources.

[b] All other income.

[c] Weighted mean ratio of AOI to LSI.

[d] Weighted mean ratio of per capita personal wealth to LSI.

ORGANIZED CRIME DEALS ITSELF IN

In addition to corrupting and enriching the Soviet officialdom at all stripes and on all levels of the hierarchy, the private wealth accumlated via the shadow economy was to have another major and fateful redistributive consequence, this time to the benefit of organized crime. With the wealth so acquired, organized crime was able to implant itself firmly throughout society in the last years of the Soviet era and, perhaps even more so, in the first post-Soviet years. It was able to bend to its own purposes much of the management, officialdom, bureaucracy, and politicians. In a phrase, its current all-permeating presence derives from the unbeatable combination of money, guns, and secure links with high places.[20]

Informed sources (see Gurov 1990 and 1995) generally place the beginning of large-scale intrusion of organized crime into the shadow economy in the 1970s.[21] Two developments converged in the 1970s. First, a large number of hardened, murderous criminals were released from Soviet prison camps, where they often had established effective organizations of their own. Second, the shadow economy achieved a high degree of prosperity combined with a high degree of vulnerability to extortion thanks to its illegal nature. In a determined and highly brutal manner, the criminal groups moved in on the fat prey for the sake of their own "original accumulation of capital"—and succeeded. Like the underground businessmen and operators before them, the criminals devoted a large part of their new wealth to buying off officials. Soon therafter, the winding down of the war in Afghanistan, the withdrawal of Soviet troops from Eastern Europe, and the general demoralization and inpoverishment of the military began releasing large quantities of weapons onto the Soviet black market. Thus enriched and armed, organized crime extended its grasp to nearly all business activities, legal as well as illegal. Today, as we know, its presence is universal, and the dividing lines between so-called mafiosi, underground operators, legitimate businessmen, government officials, the military, and politicians are anything but sharp.[22]

CONCLUDING REMARKS

How did the rapid growth of the shadow economy help bring about the collapse of a superpower, of its all-ruling Party, its formidable government, its vast economy, its awesome police and military—and, in Seurot's words in the epigraph, "without the glory of a military disaster or the tragedy of a civil war"?

We might well say with Treml and Alexeev (1994) that by the 1980s the bloated second economy reached its "dysfunctional" stage, on balance contributing (with other trends) to a loss of productivity of the whole economy. A lower than otherwise GNP growth does not *of itself* necessarily spell collapse of the economy, let alone of the whole social order. It might, though, by upsetting a preexisting domestic sociopolitical or interregional balance and the international balance (in the Soviet case, the arms race and the burden of empire)—both of which in fact happened—help bring on inflation and other disorders of the kind that were all too evident in 1989–91 as the whole Soviet order was moving toward its demise.

The Treml and Alexeev effect can be seen as a strand in a broader social scenario that takes account of parallel phenomena such as corruption, crime, and the historical dynamics of interaction between the second economy and the formal side of the Communist order. A scenario of this sort has been elaborated by Maria Los.[23] She distinguishes four "typical stages" in the life cycle of Communist states: (i) radical transformation, (ii) monopolization, (iii) reformism, and (iv) post-reformist decadence. Each stage is analyzed at some length; for brevity's sake, here we skip the first two. Suffice it to say that a Soviet-type second economy and its concomitants are already well developed in (ii). Attempts to reform the system, (iii), bring about some legalization of private activity and many new opportunities for illegal activities. Distinction between the two is increasingly blurred, while "in place of powerful control apparatus, there emerges a perception of a system of control which is erratic, corruptible, torn by contradictions and saturated by a feudal-style bureaucracy" (p. 219). Stage (iv) is marked by deepening economic crisis, weakening of the authoritarian state, and further but "barren" economic reforms:

> Typical for this stage, a forced marriage of the state- and market-economies not only heightens their . . . contradictions, but it also triggers attempts on the part of each . . . to exploit the other in a largely parasitic, politicized and economically non-competitive manner (p. 219).

A closer look at Los's stage (iv) as it played out in Communist Poland on its brink is provided by Rostowski (1990). It is the author's contention that private economic activity (both legal and illegal) is no longer a marginal phenomenon in the Polish economy. Hence,

> We are seeing the birth of a new economic system which consists of a complex network of cooperation and interpenetration, but also conflict, between the still dominant socialized sector and the various forms of private economic activity which . . . are expanding rapidly. It is . . . the decay of the socialist economic system in Poland (1990: 198).

In the ensuing discussion Rostowski devotes much attention to the growth of the "black economy" and its impact on the process of decay. In both his and Los's treatment, corruption—engendered in good measure by the second economy—plays a central role in the "decay" of the whole system.[24]

In the late 1980s the USSR still had at least a pretense of a Party-ruled Leninist polity and of a command economy. At least hardly any alternative effective structures of dominance or governance were in place. It still had to resort to the traditional Leninist instruments of rule and Stalinist tools of hierarchical economic management. But—as Jowitt (1983) perceptively argued—these were by now weakened and hollowed out by the spread of the shadow economy and of the corruption it greatly helped to bring forth. Violent organized crime weighed in somewhat earlier, while perestroika and glasnost lent a hand after 1985.

Progressively more strongly, with the wonted use of corruption, yet without formally destroying the hierarchical structure—indeed, exploiting it—the shadow economy reoriented the texture of the formal hierarchy away from its normal vertical orientation. Organized crime stepped in to apply a powerful thrust in the same direction. Within the formal structure of power, self-interest and allegiance no longer looked strictly upward. They came to be partly identified with the rapidly extending, informal, shadow, horizontal relations, webs of corrupt ties, and bureaucratic and managerial networks that compensated for the ossified vertical structure.[25] Self-interest and allegiance faced progressively downward and outward, to the founts of personal material benefit which lay within the shadow economy, in corruption, later even with organized crime. Graft and larceny became the new names of the game. The topmost authorities themselves came to look downward for self-enrichment and pressed their underlings to this end. Toward the end, uncertainty, fear, and self-preservation weighed in heavily. This process interacted with the rise of regional, ethnic, and national consciousness, responding in part to local nationalist sentiment, but also in part to inequalities of income and wealth as well as to particular economic interests.

Such sideward and downward reorientation of officials, managers, and functionaries was to acquire its ultimate rationale. When the writing on the wall appeared for most to see, not many in power were left to save the old system. The pyramid of authority had been hollowed out. Those with connections and newly appropriated capital could take cover by "retreating to previously prepared commercial positions" (Gaidar's phrase) in the new legal private economy, or in the post-Soviet shadow economy, or in organized crime, or in all of them at once.

Corrosion, corruption, and crime had done their work.

NOTES

1. Earlier versions of this piece were presented in various forums at Berkeley and in other universities and institutions in the United States, Germany, Italy, and Russia. It has also appeared as Working Paper 2.63 in the series Political Relations and Institutions Research Group: Europe East and West—Challenges to Sovereignty from Above and Below, Centers for German and European Studies and for Slavic and East European Studies, University of California, Berkeley. The valuable criticisms and comments offered in those occasions are gratefully acknowledged, as is the separate advice and encouragement by Professor V. G. Treml (Duke University). Also gratefully noted is research support for this study by the University of

California at Berkeley and its Centers for Slavic and East European Studies and German and European Studies. All responsibility rests with the author.

2. See, for example, Castells and Kiselyova (1995); Dallin (1992); editors' introduction to Ellman and Kontorovich, eds. (1992); Goldman (1982); Schroeder (1998); Seurot (1996); Treml (1993). Here we bypass the related issue as to whether the Soviet-type command economy was a "stable" or "viable" system; it *did* fall—and has not risen again.

3. A casual calculation suggests that for 7–8 years, on average the USSR gained from the energy price windfall the equivalent of about one percentage point of additional GNP growth per year, a significant benefit. And yet, the decline in the annual rate of GNP continued.

4. Regarding the "shielding" effect of the limited legalization of individual economic activity: personal conversations in the USSR with underground producers and dealers, December 1987. Zubakin (1994) is particularly informative regarding the instrumental use of cooperatives and similar innovations for insider enrichment. He dates the sudden explosion of this practice at 1989.

5. Important instances of legal private economic activity in the USSR are, first and foremost, private plots at the socialized farms and the "garden plots" of urban dwellers and the private sale of their produce; private and cooperative home ownership. Less important but not trivial were the significant (but in the West often neglected) individuals and groups engaged in mining and hunting, various medical practitioners, certain teachers, and lawyers (*advokaty*) and notaries serving the public at large. Toward the end of the Soviet era the advokaty alone numbered around 28,000.

6. Unlike our concept of the second economy, the Soviet perception of the shadow economy often includes the private gain from cooking the books of official entities, an elusive but considerable magnitude.

7. A detailed first-hand account of the trials triggered by this campaign by one of the defense attorneys is in Evel'son (1986). A shorter first-hand account is in Simis (1982).

8. An early bird's-eye view of the Soviet second economy appears in Grossman (1977). Varieties and techniques of illicit activity are briefly described in Grossman (1979). Clark (1993) is particularly good on the attendant corruption of officialdom. Further references in Grossman (1990). With regard to prospects for economic reform during the perestroika era, the second economy probably cut both ways, as discussed in Grossman (1989).

9. A summary account of this episode and other manifestations of the shadow economy in Central Asia appears in Rumer (1989: ch. 8). A more poignant assessment of the cotton affair is in Timofeev (1993: 200–206). An extensive personal account by the senior investigator of the affair, with particular emphasis on alleged implication of very high persons in Moscow, is Gdlian and Ivanov (1994). The ensuing politically charged "Gdlian [Gdlyan] and Ivanov case" is assessed in Clark (1993: 191ff.); see also Vaksberg (1991: 213) and Handelman (1995: 94–95).

10. A very useful collection of essays on the second economy in ten "Marxist" states, ranging from the Soviet Union and China to Nicaragua and Tanzania, together with the editor's important introductory and concluding chapters, is in Los (1990).
11. Soviet law provided, in addition to the state-owned sector, for a variety of other "socialist" entities, which were wholly or partly devoted to economic activity as well—namely, collective farms, cooperatives, and so-called social (*obshchestvennye*) organizations. The last category included the CP and the Komsomol, the official trade unions, down to local sports or theater groups. The Western literature on their legal-economic status is sparse; a notable exception is Ajani (1988). In the aggregate, the economic functions and asset holdings of the nonstate socialist entities in the USSR were very large, as was their role in the shadow economy.
12. Everyday living in Soviet-type societies required continuous coping with shortages and other frustrations. Much of this coping was within the bounds of the legal, but much was not, though in the latter case enforcement was lax or spotty. Exchange of favors played an important role here (though, unfortunately, ignored by economic analysis). Information on coping is large and in many languages. A very good inside account by an anthropologist on Poland in the early 1980s is Wedel (1986). See also the collective volume, Wedel, ed. (1992). The latter includes an interesting contemporaneous piece on corruption and the shadow economy in Poland under German occupation by K. Wyka.
13. On a more modest scale, the loot chain appears 150 years ago in Nikolai Gogol's *Dead Souls* (first edition, 1842), as the hero, Chichikov, settles down to the life of a corrupt middle-ranking official in the Tsar's service.
14. Note that in the West stolen goods generally fetch less than their legitimate counterparts.
15. Koriagina (1990 and 1991: 27–44). A survey and analysis of Soviet research on the Soviet shadow economy, and particularly of Koriagina's work, by one of the earliest Soviet researchers of the problem is Rutgaizer (1992).
16. Treml and Alexeev (1994).
17. The reader is referred to Matthews (1978). Lidiia Shatunovskaia describes in her reminiscences (1982) how the arrival in Moscow of trainloads of "liberated" valuables from abroad at the end of World War II created a large and lasting black market in such objects among the highly privileged, of whom she was then one.
18. I am indebted to Aron Katsenelinboigen for this point (personal communication).
19. Simis (1982): ch. 3, "The District Mafia," presents an interesting picture of the provincial elite, which, lacking the privileges of its counterparts in the capitals, generated corruption and the shadow economy in its home towns in the course of minding its own benefits.

20. This is not the occasion to take stock of the place and power of organized crime in present-day Russia and the Commonwealth of Independent States (CIS), nor to recount its long and tangled history. The literature on Soviet/Russian organized crime and "mafia" is now quite large, yet by the very topic, often of uncertain reliability. The following are a few of the more important publications relied upon here, with particular attention to the link to the shadow economy: Frisby (1998); Handelman (1995); Lesnik and Blanc (1990); the special issue of *Demokratizatsiya* (1994), edited and partly authored by Louise I. Shelley; Gdlian and Ivanov (1994) (on the cotton fraud and its patronage in highest places, by two senior procuratorial investigators); works by Alexander I. Gurov, a leading specialist formerly at the USSR Ministry of Internal Affairs (1990 and 1995); and, among her other works, Shelley (1994).
21. Notably, the Berkeley-Duke open-ended interviews with former underground businessmen and other informed persons, which pertained to as late a period as the end of the 1970s, brought out no mention of extortion by organized crime—despite frequent mention of extortion by corrupt Party, police, and other officials. Nor was there reference to enforcement of contracts by criminal violence. Enforcement by nonviolent means (arbitration, ostracism) was mentioned. On later violent intrusion of organized crime into shadow economy business, see Razinkin (1995).
22. For informative recent overviews of the melding of organized crime and business see Kryshtanovskaya (1995: 591–614) and Sundiev (1995: 615–34).
23. Concluding chapter in Los (1990). Also apposite is her introductory chapter.
24. A valuable complement to the just discussed Polish case are three important works on Hungary under communism. Seleny (1994) deals with the implications which the scholarly study of the Hungarian "secondary" economy, ongoing in 1978–82, bore for the system's future and the related debate within the Party itself. Rupp (1983) provides an instructive first-hand account of the semi-sub-rosa private enterprise in the countryside under communism. Szelenyi (1988) addresses at length and in depth the process of "interrupted [rural] *embourgeoisement*" and its relation to the overall system.
25. There is a Russian literature on informal networks within the formal hierarchy during the late Soviet years, associated with such names as Leonid Grigor'ev, Vitalii Naishul', and Sergei Pavlenko.

REFERENCES

BDOP. *Berkeley-Duke Occasional Papers on the Second Economy in the Soviet Union.*

Ajani, Gianmaria. 1988. *La proprietà delle organizzazioni sociali nel diritto dei paesi socialisti.* Milan: Giuffrè.

Castells, Manuel, and Emma Kiselyova. 1995. *The Collapse of Soviet Communism: A View from the Information Society.* Berkeley: International and Area Studies.

Clark, William A. 1993. *Crime and Punishment of Soviet Officialdom: Combating Corruption in the Political Elite, 1965–1990.* Armonk, N.Y.: Sharpe.

Dallago, Bruno. 1990. *The Irregular Economy.* Aldershot: Dartmouth.

Dallin, Alexander. 1992. "Causes of the Collapse of the USSR." *Post-Soviet Affairs* 8, 4: 279–302.

Demokratizatsiya: The Journal of Post-Soviet Democratization (Washington, D.C.). Special issue, Summer 1994. Edited and partly written by Louise I. Shelley.

Ellman, Michael, and Vladimir Kontorovich, eds. 1992. *The Disintergration of the Soviet Economic System.* London: Routledge.

Frisby, Tanya. 1998. "The Rise of Organized Crime in Russia: Its Roots and Social Significance." *Europe-Asia Studies* 50, 1 (January): 27–50.

Gdlian, Tel'man, and Nikoilai Ivanov. 1994. *Kremlevskoe delo* [The Kremlin affair]. Rostov.

Goldman, Marshall I. 1994. *The USSR in Crisis: The Failure of an Economic System.* N.Y.: Norton, 1982.

Grachev, Andrei. 1994. *Kremlevskaia khronika* [Kremlin chronicle]. Moscow: Eksmo.

Grossman, Gregory. 1977. "The 'Second Economy' in the USSR." *Problems of Communism* 26, 5 (October–November). Reprinted in *The Soviet Economy: Continuity and Change,* ed. Morris Bornstein. Boulder: Westview, 1981.

————. 1979. "Notes on the Illegal Private Economy and Corruption." In U.S. Congress, Joint Economic Committee, *The Soviet Economy in a Time of Change,* pp. 834–55. Washington, D.C.: Government Printing Office.

————. 1989. "The Second Economy: Boon or Bane for the Reform of the First Economy." In *Economic Reform in the Socialist World,* ed. Stanislaw Gomulka, Y. C. Ha, and C. O. Kim. New York: Macmillan.

————. 1990. "The Second Economy in the USSR and Eastern Europe: A Bibliography." *BDOP,* no. 21 (July).

Gurov, Alexander I. 1990. *Professional'naia prestupnost'* [Crime as profession]. Moscow.

————. 1995. *Krasnaia mafiia* [Red Mafia]. Moscow.

Handelman, Stephen. 1995. *Comrade Criminal: Russia's New Mafiya*. New Haven: Yale University Press.

Jowitt, Ken. 1983. "Neotraditionalism: The Political Corruption of a Leninist Regime." *Soviet Studies* 35, 3 (July): 275–97.

Kennan, George F. 1947. "The Sources of Soviet Conduct." *Foreign Affairs* 25, 4 (July): 566–82.

Koriagina, Tat'iana I. 1990. "Tenevaia ekonomika v SSSR" [The shadow economy in the USSR]. *Voprosy ekonomiki* 3.

————. 1991. "Analiz, otsenki, prognozy" [Analysis, estimates, prognoses]. In Ulybin, ed., pp. 26–44.

Kotkin, Stephen. 1997. "In Search of the Nomenklatura." *East European Constitutional Review,* Fall, pp. 104–20.

Kryshtanovskaya, Olga. 1995. "Russia's Illegal Structures." In Segbers and De Spiegeleire, eds., pp. 591–614.

Lesnik, Renata, and H. Blanc. 1990. *L'Empire corrompu*. Paris: Lafonte.

Los, Maria. 1990. *The Second Economy in Marxist States*. New York: St. Martin's.

Matthews, Mervyn. 1978. *Privilege in the Soviet Union: A Study of Elite Life-Styles under Communism*. London: George Allen and Unwin, 1978.

Millar, James R., and Sharon L. Wolchik, eds. 1994. *The Social Legacy of Communism*. Washington, D.C.: Woodrow Wilson Center Press.

Mr. X. *See* Kennan.

Razinkin, V. S. 1995. "Vory v zakone" i prestupnye klany [Criminals-within-the-code and criminal clans], Moscow: Association for Criminology.

Rostowski, Jacek. 1990. "The Decay of Socialism and the Growth of Private Enterprise in Poland." In *Polish Paradoxes,* ed. Stanislaw Gomulka and Antony Polonsky. London: Routledge.

Rumer, Boris. 1989. *Soviet Central Asia: A Tragic Experiment*. Boston: Unwin Hyman.

Rupp, Kalman. 1983. *Entrepreneurs in Red*. Albany: SUNY Press.

Rutgaizer, Valerii M. 1992. "The Shadow Economy in the USSR." *BDOP,* no. 34 (February).

Schroeder, Gertrude. 1998. "The Soviet Economy and the Fate of the USSR." In *The Collapse of the Soviet Union,* ed. Mark Kramer. New York: Praeger.

Segbers, Klaus, and Stephan De Spiegeleire, eds. 1995. *Post-Soviet Puzzles: Mapping the Political Economy of the Former Soviet Union,* vol. 3. Baden-Baden: Nomos.

Seleny, Anna. 1994. "Constructing the Discourse of Transformation: Hungary, 1979–82." *East European Politics and Societies* 8, 3 (Fall).

Seurot, François. 1996. *Les Causes économiques de la fin de l'Empire soviétique*. Paris: Presses Universitaires de France.

Shatunovskaia, Lidiia. 1982. *Zhizn' v Kremle* [Life in the Kremlin]. New York: Chalidze.

Shelley, Louise I. 1994. "Crime and the Collapse of the Soviet State." In Millar and Wolchik, eds.

Simis, Konstantin. 1982. *USSR: The Corrupt Society.* New York: Simon and Schuster.

Solnik, Steven L. 1996. "The Breakdown of Hierarchies in the Soviet Union and China: A Neo-Institutional Perspective." *World Politics* 48 (January): 209–38.

Sundiev, Igor'. 1995. "Criminological Components of the Current Social Dynamics in Russia." In Segbers and De Spiegeleire, eds., pp. 615–34.

Szelenyi, Ivan. 1988. *Socialist Entrepreneurs: Embourgeoisement in Rural Hungary.* Madison: University of Wisconsin Press.

Timofeev, Lev. 1993. *Chernyi rynok kak politicheskaia sistema* [The black market as a political system]. Vilnius: VIMO.

Treml, Vladimir G. 1993. "Debate: Why Did the Soviet Economic System Collapse? Two Schools of Thought." *RFE/RL Research Report* 2, 23 (4 June): 53–55.

Treml, Vladimir G., and Michael Alexeev. 1994. "The Growth of the Second Economy in the Soviet Union and Its Impact on the System." In *The Post-Communist Economic Transformation,* ed. Robert W. Campbell. Boulder: Westview. The full version of the paper, entitled "The Second Economy and the Destabilizing Effect of Its Growth on the State Economy of the Soviet Union, 1965–1989," is in *BDOP,* no. 36 (December 1993).

Ulybin, K. A., ed. 1991. *Tenevaia ekonomika* [Shadow economy]. Moscow: Ekonomika.

Vaksberg, Arkady. 1991. *The Soviet Mafia.* London: Weidenfeld and Nicolson.

Wedel, Janine. 1986. *The Private Poland.* New York: Facts on File.

————. 1992. *The Unplanned Society: Poland during and after Communism.* New York: Columbia University Press.

Zubakin, V. 1994. "'Vtoraia ekonomika'" [The "Second Economy"]. *Voprosy ekonomiki* 11: 156–60.

POLITICAL SURVIVAL OR ENTREPRENEURIAL DEVELOPMENT? OBSERVATIONS ON RUSSIAN BUSINESS NETWORKS

Peter Huber and Andreas Wörgötter[1]

Networks are hybrid forms between hierarchies and markets. The present article focuses on the structure of Russian business networks and their potential for integration into European business networks. In Russia, two competing types of networks can currently be identified: *survival networks* and *entrepreneurial networks*. In the latter, the main interests of the enterprise managers are to improve market performance and profits. But in the former, enterprise managers are involved in a large "rent-seeking" game, in which political and market power are the major means by which rents are extracted. Managers within survival networks evaluate both internal and external business relationships with reference to their effects on rent-extraction capacities. In Russia today, survival networks predominate and entrepreneurial networks are relatively few in number.

BUSINESS NETWORKS IN A "NORMAL" ENVIRONMENT

In institutional economics, attention to networks has been driven by the realization that many innovations are taking place primarily in the space between markets and hierarchies (Lindenberg 1996). Many phrases have been used to describe these hybrid forms: symbiotic contracts (Schanze 1993); networks (Williamson 1991); clans (Ouchi 1980). Business networks, which we define as sets of connected exchange relationships between actors controlling business activities, have been interpreted as important contributors to regional development and as determinants of the comparative advantage of nations (Porter 1990).

The business relationships that comprise networks may differ in form, such as whether they are based on trade or capital ties. The relationships may also differ in content, such as whether they are based on common technologies, knowledge, administrative routines, or social ties. Moreover, business relationships tend to be highly complex, involving more than one activity and requiring substantial efforts to resolve the conflicts that inevitably arise. Then too the bases of relationships tend to change over time; indeed, mutual adaptation of the partners is typical, as a result of which cooperation may be reduced, intensified, or shifted to new bases. On the whole, though, and notwithstanding these adaptations, business relationships in mature economies tend to be relatively stable.[2]

Why do such networks arise? A number of theories have been advanced. Transaction costs theory (Williamson 1975) holds that networks arise as a special institutional arrangement—governance structure or mechanism of cooperation—for handling problems that combine asset specificity, bounded rationality, and human opportunism.[3] Williamson (1991) argues that the particular advantage of networks over other methods of coordinating human economic activities (such as hierarchies and markets) is that they minimize transaction costs in cases of medium asset specificity and a high need for flexibility.

Empirical research has gone part of the way toward confirming this hypothesis. Business networks have been more prevalent in industries that require high flexibility—due to rapidly developing markets—and substantial human capital. Examples include networks of universities and biochemical enterprises (Powell 1996) and the consumer electronics industry (Ernst 1995). Networks are also more prevalent in cases in which producers have found innovative ways to upgrade standardized products by linking themselves to upstream enterprises through the creation of limited asset specificity. Examples include woodworking and pulp-processing networks spanning Denmark and Sweden (Hakanson and Snehota 1995) and quality-label poultry in France (Menard 1996). At the same time, empirical research has qualified Williamson's hypothesis. The original architecture of networks is often influenced heavily by such factors as enterprise culture, history, and the institutional background available during the process of creation. Thus, Zysman (1995) has found that networks in Southeast Asia and the United States differ substantially between nations with respect to their openness and verticality—that is, the ease with which networks are penetrated by outsiders and the extent to which they are organized as groups of social peers.[4]

NETWORKS IN THE RUSSIAN ECONOMY

Networks emerge within concrete cultural, historical, and institutional environments and are subject to continuous evolutionary change. The context within which they have arisen in Russia is quite different from that in mature market economies, which should lead us to expect their structure and consequences to be different as well.

HISTORICAL CONTEXT

Networks in transition economies predate the collapse of communism. They were formed during the era of state planning, products of both the trade relationships of that era and the unofficial ties that emerged within the gray and black markets. But the nature of the networks was different from those in mature market economies owing to the extremely hierarchical nature of central planning, the absence of prices as means of generating meaningful information, and the exclusive concentration on quantity of production (Hirschhausen and Hsui 1995). Organized around territorial industrial complexes, official relationships between firms mainly served delivery functions. Joint ventures in research and licensing relationships—characteristic of business networks in mature market economies—were almost completely lacking. And to mitigate the costs of planning, transactions between firms were highly integrated horizontally, such that the number of transactions was relatively small (Rühl 1995).

The networks that derived from the gray and black markets were also distinctive. Relationships within these markets were based on personal ties, such as friendship, rather than on impersonal business ties. While the authorities tolerated these networks, they also eyed them with suspicion. Accordingly, the networks had to be less formal and more conspiratorial than those which predominate in market economies.

Substantial empirical evidence concerning corporate structures and financial-industrial groups (FIGs) in Russia suggests that relationships forged under the planning system remain operative, especially in large-scale industry. Thus, according to Gorbatova (1995), banks that had once channeled export financing and credits to industrial enterprises have remained closely linked to those enterprises even after their organizational devolution, and in some cases emerged as owners of those firms. Similarly, Gurkov and Asselsberg (1995) found that as of 1994, old, excessively long transport routes for products were still being used, despite their economic irrationality.[5] Finally, historical continuity has been maintained by the privatization of the former departments (*glavki*) of ministries. These were transformed into joint stock companies; they now provide consultancy and export services to their former clientele (Starodubrovskaia 1995).[6]

Some evidence also exists of price discrimination by old networks against new ones. Dolgopiatova and Evseyeva (1995), for example, found that in 1993, 10 percent of the managers of state-owned enterprises that they interviewed refused to work with managers of private firms, and 45.7 percent stated that they would do so only under dire necessity.

At the same time, newly founded enterprises are building new networks of their own. Freinkman (1995) argued that the underground enterprises (*tsekhi*) founded during the Gorbachev era usually had good connections to both criminal and political circles and may have served as points for the crystallization of new network structures.

PRODUCTION PROCESSES

One legacy of the planned economy was a production structure in which enterprises were unusually large relative to the resource markets in which they were located. Russian enterprises, accordingly, differ from American counterparts less in their total size than in their level of concentration (Joskow, Schmalensee, and Tsukanova 1994). An extreme example is Krasnoyarsk *kray.* Of the ten towns with more than ten thousand inhabitants, six are dominated by one producer, employing more than 40 percent of the townships' workforce. Indeed, for many of these towns the next possibility for employment is several hundred kilometers away (Huber, Nagaev, and Wörgötter 1996). Although Krasnoyark is extreme, the phenomenon is widespread. This means that in many Russian localities, there will not be enough diversity of enterprises to support the construction of new networks.

This monopsonistic position of firms on labor markets has additional implications. They can get away with not paying workers their overdue wages, even when the enterprises are profitable.[7] They have a strong influence on regional politics, due in part to their contributions to regional budgets.[8] But because these firms are also highly dependent on the localities in which they produce, they will feel threatened by the entry of new enterprises into the region—even in sectors that do not compete directly with the indigenous firms—because new entrants will weaken the strategic positions of firms in regional input markets. Then too managers of large enterprises use these as bases of power for activities outside the enterprise that serve as major sources of income. Thus, in 1994, the majority of managers of formerly state-owned enterprises owned a multitude of firms (Gurkov and Asselsberg 1995). Similarly, Bim (1996) found that 73 percent of managers interviewed admitted to owning firms that were either deliverers or suppliers to the very firm they managed. It is not surprising, therefore, that harassment of new firms is a common phenomenon in these regions. Given these orientations, we find little organization of production on the basis of relatively open and nonhierarchical networks.

A second feature likely to influence the nature of emerging networks in Russia lies in the production structure of Russian industry itself. The typical Russian producer is an enterprise that is horizontally integrated, located in heavy industry and/or mass production of standardized goods, and uses relatively few specific assets. Such a technological profile is not well suited to network creation, unlike, for example, the electronics producers of Central Asia or other instances of production that foster cross-border networks.

The environment surrounding the firms is also less supportive of network creation than is the case in mature market economies.

The socialist enterprise itself provided most services, whether these were social or producer (such as auditing). This applied in particular to the organization of financial relationships. The result is that in Russia, in many instances, banks are heavily dependent on, or directly belong to, the enterprises for which they organize trade.

THE INSTITUTIONAL ENVIRONMENT

The institutional environment of firms gives additional impetus to the maintenance of survival networks and efforts to monopolize entry. The stark realities of transition make clear to Russian managers where their interests lie. Certain institutional changes are clear threats to their political and material security, and they will use their powers to prevent them.[9] Rühl (1995), for example, has argued that the inter-enterprise arrears crisis is sustained by enterprise managers' knowledge of their power to induce the central government repeatedly to bail them out.

This willingness to use their powers to tilt balances in their favor is reinforced by the knowledge that most decisions taken during the transition have long-term implications. Hence, even if some costs are associated with the exertion of power, the long-run gains—or loss-avoidance—may be very large. Moreover, the lack of a fixed, consistent institutional and legal framework makes it almost impossible to abstain from the power-political game or to stay within the bounds of legality when conducting business. The inevitable legal breaches allow actors to compromise even those unwilling to play at the power game.

TYPES OF RUSSIAN BUSINESS NETWORKS

As noted, we divide networks in Russia into two ideal types: survival and entrepreneurial.[10] Survival networks encompass enterprises that see little future for themselves in competitive market conditions; indeed, they are formed with the explicit goal of isolating participants from market competition. The purpose of the network is short-term rent extraction from the government—i.e., lobbying. The network structure is based on ties created during the socialist era. Entrepreneurial networks, by contrast, are composed of actors that seek to compete in the new markets by developing economically viable activities. Two types of entrepreneurial networks can be identified: those that build on old structures and those composed of new structures.[11] Survival and entrepreneurial networks differ with respect to their architecture and their orientation toward cooperation with new foreign partners and toward the marketization process in Russia today.

SURVIVAL NETWORKS

The predominant goal of actors within survival networks is to protect or maximize their power to extract rents, which can be quite large in the conditions of Russia today. Those rents may be used to gain riches, to avert bankruptcy, or both. Moreover, since increasing one's power requires dedicated followers and since the allegiance of a new member is always hard to assess, survival networks will be relatively closed. And since increasing power also requires substantial control over the power base, survival networks will also be highly vertical. Finally, survival networks favor stability of membership and relationships over time.

The attitude toward interaction with foreigners is ambivalent. On the one hand, foreign participation can be a source of new financing, which can often be deflected for private use. On the other hand, Western foreign firms are interested in profits and typically seek to impose controls that endanger the ability of network members to extract rents from their enterprises. The preferred interaction with foreign firms, therefore, especially on the part of actors in the top levels of the network, is trade.

ENTREPRENEURIAL NETWORKS

The driving force behind entrepreneurial networks is profit-motivated actors. Some of these are actors recruited from old enterprises who believe their firms are capable of being restructured and made profitable. Others are new entrants: enterprises founded by actors previously not involved in the power game within the socialist economy.

Genuinely new firms are quite rare in Russia; most new entrants are products of the splitting up of state-owned enterprises and changes in legal forms. In addition to being relatively few in number, entrepreneurial networks based on new entrants are quite disadvantaged in the power struggle. They are led by individuals with limited experience and are not well positioned to defend themselves politically. Consequently, networks composed of these actors tend to be unstable, open, and horizontal. Entrepreneurial networks therefore look to foreign partners to help them survive despite their disadvantages; any form of cooperation and activity from abroad is welcome to these actors. Yet, as stand-alone institutions, they are usually too weak to prosper or survive in the conditions of Russia today.

Entrepreneurial networks based on old structures are better positioned, however. They are led by individuals who are more experienced and who have a historic, more stable power base. Relative to survival networks and new entrepreneurial networks, they are marked by intermediate levels of openness and verticality of architecture. They are open to foreign cooperation to the extent that it enhances their profitability and their capacity to restructure existing enterprises. Since the latter requires substantial capital, they prefer foreign direct investment to other forms of cooperation.

THE EVOLUTION OF NETWORK TYPES

Which kinds of networks are established in any given region depends on the interests of the managers of industrial enterprises in that region and the power base available to the actors within the network. In regions in which very few firms dominated input and output markets before economic reform, those firms retain the power to harass new entrants by discriminating against them on markets and by intervening against them in politics. In Russia today, the degree of monopolization and monopsonization varies greatly across regions and industries. Thus, while the situation in Krasnoyarsk is very well suited to rent-extraction activities, other regions are marked by much less industrial concentration.[12] This is apparent from aggregate data. Huber, Nagaev, and Wörgötter (1997), constructing *herfindahl* indexes covering the regions of Russia and twelve industries within those regions, find that the indicator varies from 0.65 to 0.12. Similarly, industries differ substantially in their concentration statistics. Some industries are heavily localized in one region, such as nonferrous metallurgy in Krasnoyarsk and fuel in Tyumen'. Others have no such geographical specialization (Huber, Nagaev, and Wörgötter 1996b).

Whether managers are inclined to enter survivalist networks is predominantly a function of their expectations of the future. Actors who see few chances of surviving in the new circumstances will be more prone to adopt a survivalist stance than those who see some future for their enterprise. However, other factors may enter into the calculation as well. Within survival networks, there is a clear center-periphery dimension to the rent-extraction process. The old, now privatized departments (glavki) of the industrial ministries in the center usually control both foreign trade and the network itself. Thus, the center extracts much of the rent that might otherwise have gone to local actors. This may tempt actors in the periphery to opt out of the survivalist network, but such defection has its costs. For example, in the forestry sector, most of the transport facilities remain under the control of the center, and discriminatory pricing, also a prerogative of the center, can make products from the periphery uncompetitive in international markets.

Given the huge reduction in output in Russia during the past decade and given the incidence of concentration that provides a power base, it is not surprising that survival networks are the predominant form in Russia today. But what of the future? It seems obvious that from an evolutionary standpoint, a strategy concerned primarily with reducing the value of existing assets is not fit to survive in the long run. This would favor the eventual strengthening of entrepreneurial networks. Indeed, state-owned firms have already begun to notice that new private customers are more reliable in meeting their payments. The real question is how long existing survivalist networks can be expected to survive. We suspect that Russian networks will evolve into an entrepreneurial form only over a very long period of time. The time frame may be shorter in regions and sectors in which industry is least concentrated. But for the most part, the size of the rents still to be distributed is large, as is the ingenuity and persistence of the actors operating within survivalist networks.

INTEGRATION INTO INTERNATIONAL NETWORKS

The integration of Russia into international production networks will remain a difficult task and may fail altogether. Most Russian partners will assess agreements principally in terms of the impact on their position in the internal struggle for power and the impact on their capacity to continue extracting rents. Foreign owners who emphasize profitability endanger the rent-extraction process. This bodes ill for joint ventures. Projects that are concerned with employment reduction will also face opposition from survivalist networks. Activities geared toward upstream or downstream cooperation in existing markets are more difficult to achieve than activities geared toward selling products in new markets. Integration is also hampered by technological realities: large Russian enterprises are generally not flexible in their production processes and do not specialize in technologically advanced products.

The regional distribution of foreign direct investments as a percentage of total investments in the Russian Federation is indicative of the conditions beneficial to such investments. A clear industrial-geographical pattern emerges. Oil-rich Tyumen' leads with 17.86 percent of the total, and its two autonomous districts, which are also oil-rich, stand immediately behind. The capital city of Moscow, a "port of entry," follows with 11.97 percent of the investments. The other places in which capital investments were clustered were either regions that experienced relatively small output declines during the transition (Samara, Chelyabinsk, Bashkortostan) or that are relatively rich in resources (Sakha Yakut, Irkutsk) or that are located close to the sea (Caucasus) (Wörgötter 1997). As for the sectoral distribution of foreign direct investments, as of April 1995, 17.66 percent of all foreign investments had gone into the fuel industry (Stern 1996), making it the second largest branch in this respect after domestic trade. The forestry industry is the third largest recipient.

European networks are not the only option for Russian enterprises. The Commonwealth of Independent States and/or the Russian Far East are also potential loci of integration. At present, all three regions have been objects of such network creation. Such creation follows clear regional and sectoral patterns, often dictated by the transportation costs of products. Siberian regions, for example, have developed close ties to East Asian countries (Tak 1994a, 1994b; Obersteiner 1995).

CONCLUSION

Survivalist networks, which predominate in Russia, tend to be closed and hierarchical. When entering Russian business networks, foreigners must anticipate that their welcome will depend strongly on the effects of their presence on the rent-extraction capacities of existing enterprise managers. This stands in sharp contrast to the international business networks observed in most Western countries, in the design of which profitability is the main goal; these tend to be substantially more open and less hierarchical in their structure. Thus, any efforts to incorporate Russian firms into European networks face major obstacles. Entrance costs into Russian producer networks are high since time is needed to understand the highly complex internal structures. Largely for internal power reasons, Russian partners often fail to negotiate mutually favorable agreements and fail to show flexibility in their dealings. The goals of Russian managers working in survival networks will often diverge fundamentally from those of Western partners working in entrepreneurial networks. Given these differences in structure and interests, it is quite possible that Russian networks will remain relatively secluded from European networks and that existing network structures in Russia will become instruments largely for preserving the institutional status quo in that country.

To be sure, countervailing tendencies exist. In some areas of the Russian economy, entrepreneurial networks are more frequently found. In economically less powerful regions and industries, with smaller-scale enterprises producing food and other consumer products, networks tend to be less hierarchical, more open, more profit-oriented, and more flexible. Currently, the number and importance of such networks are relatively low. But in the long run, competitive forces are at work that may help them to proliferate.

NOTES

1. This article originally appeared in *Post-Soviet Affairs* 14, 1 (January– March 1998): 81–91. It is reprinted here with permission from *Post-Soviet Affairs.*©V. H. Winston & Son, Inc., 360 South Ocean Boulevard, Palm Beach, Fla. 33480. All rights reserved.
2. Hakansson and Snehota (1995), for example, report that more than 70 percent of the suppliers of large companies in Sweden did not change over a ten-year period.
3. Asset specificity refers to the degree to which a particular asset is specific to one particular relationship and cannot be used in potential alternative relationships. High asset specificity thus gives rise to situations of bilateral monopoly.
4. For a similar typology, see Park (1996).
5. However, they also found that this was not ubiquitous and that many enterprises had changed their customers.
6. For more on financial-industrial groups in Russia, see Johnson (1997).
7. Although Krasnoyarsk has the third highest profit rate among Russian krays, it also has the fifth highest rate of unpaid wages (Huber, Nagaev, and Wörgötter 1996a).
8. In Tomsk, for example, 80 percent of the budget revenues to the *oblast'* administration come from one oil-producing firm (Tomskneft); see Huber, Nagaev, and Wörgötter (forthcoming).
9. Frey (1977) has argued that constitutional questions can be solved only under a veil of ignorance, in which it is not clear whether a particular member of society will profit or lose from a particular agreement.
10. Starodubrovskaia (1995) refers to "survival" and "developmental" financial-industrial groups. We stress that ours are ideal types which do not exist in pure form. In the real world, elements of both types may well be mixed within a given network. However, real-world networks may be distinguished by the predominance of one or the other element.
11. This division is also ideal-typical since old and new entrepreneurial networks interact and form alliances. The distinction, however, usefully highlights the fact that old structures are quite diverse and are not necessarily survivalist. For examples, see Prokop (1995).
12. On Tomsk, see Huber, Nagaev, and Wörgötter (forthcoming).

REFERENCES

Bim, Alexander S. 1996. "Ownership, Control over the Enterprises, and Strategies of Stockholders." Laxenburg, Austria: International Institute for Applied Systems Analysis (IIASA). IIASA Working Paper WP-96-050.

Dolgopiatova, Tatyana, and Irina Evseyeva. 1995. "The Behavior of Russian Industrial Enterprises under Transformation." *Communist Economies and Economic Transformation* 7, 3: 319–31.

Ernst, Dieter. 1995. "New Opportunities and Challenges for Taiwan's Electronics Industry: The Role of International Cooperation." Berkeley: Berkeley Roundtable on the International Economy (BRIE), University of California. BRIE Working Paper No. 78.

Freinkman, Lev. 1995. "Financial-Industrial Groups in Russia: Emergence of Large Diversified Companies." *Communist Economies and Economic Transformation* 7, 1: 51–67.

Frey, Bruno S. 1977. *Moderne Politische Ökonomie.* Zurich: Piper.

Gorbatova, Larisa. 1995. "Formation of Connections between Finance and Industry in Russia: Basic Strategies and Form." *Communist Economies and Economic Transformation* 7, 1: 21–34.

Gurkov, Igor B., and Gary Asselsberg. 1995. "Ownership and Control in Russian Privatized Companies: Evidence from a Survey." *Communist Economies and Economic Transformation* 7, 2: 195–211.

Hakansson, Hakan, and Ivan Snehota. 1995. *Developing Relations in Business Networks.* London and New York: Routledge.

Hirschhausen, Christian von, and Wan-Sze Hsui. 1995. "Industrial Restructuring in the Baltic Countries: Large Scale Privatization, New Enterprise Networks and Growing Diversity of Corporate Governance." *Communist Economies and Economic Transformation* 7, 4: 421–43.

Huber, Peter; Sergei Nagaev; and Andreas Wörgötter. 1996a. *Krasnoyarsk: A Region-Based Approach to Industrial Restructuring.* Paris: OECD.

————. 1996b. "The Relocation of Russian Industry, 1987–1993." Laxenburg, Austria: IIASA. IIASA Working Paper 96-162.

————. 1997. "Regional Industrial Output in Russia, 1987–1993." Laxenburg, Austria: IIASA. Unpublished manuscript.

————. Forthcoming. "Tomsk Regional Report." Paris: OECD.

Johnson, Juliet. 1997. "Russia's Emerging Financial-Industrial Groups." *Post-Soviet Affairs* 13, 4 (October–December): 333–65.

Joskow, Paul L.; Richard Schmalensee; and Natalia Tsukanova. 1994. "Competition Policy in Russia during and after Privatization." *Brookings Papers on Economic Activity.* Washington, D.C.: Brookings Institution.

Lindenberg, Siegwart. 1996. "Multiple-Tie Networks, Structural Tendencies and Path Dependence: Another Look at Hybrid Forms of Governance." *Journal of Institutional and Theoretical Economics* 152, 1: 188–96.

Menard, Claude. 1996. "On Clusters, Hybrids and Other Strange Forms: The Case of the French Poultry Industry." *Journal of Institutional and Thoeretical Economics* 152, 1: 154–88.

Obersteiner, Michael. 1995. "Status and Structure of the Forest Industry in Siberia." Laxenburg, Austria: IIASA. IIASA Working Paper 95-30.

Ouchi, William G. 1980. "Markets, Bureaucracies and Clans." *Administrative Science Quarterly* 25, 1: 129–41.

Park, Sueng Ho. 1996. "Managing an Interorganizational Network: A Framework of the Institutional Mechanism of Network Control." *Organization Studies* 17, 5: 795–824.

Porter, Michael E. 1990. *The Competitive Advantage of Nations*. New York: Macmillan.

Powell, Walter W. 1996. "Inter-Organizational Collaboration in the Biotechnology Industry." *Journal of Institutional and Theoretical Economics* 152, 1: 226–43.

Prokop, Jane E. 1995. "Industrial Conglomerates, Risk-Spreading and the Transition in Russia." *Communist Economies and Economic Transformation* 7, 1: 35–49.

Rühl, Christof. 1995. "Privatization and Corporate Control." Los Angeles: University of California. Unpublished manuscript.

Schanze, Erich. 1993. "Symbiotic Contracts." *Journal of Institutional and Theoretical Economics* 149, 4: 691–97.

Starodubrovskaia, Irina. 1995. "Financial-Industrial Groups: Illusions and Realities." *Communist Economies and Economic Transformation* 7, 1: 5–19.

Stern, Richard E. 1996. "Policy Analysis of Foreign Direct Investments into the Russian Federation: A Study of the Current State of Affairs and Prospects for the Future." Vienna: Institute for Advanced Studies. East European Series, Working Paper No. 34.

Tak, Kwang-Il. 1994a. "Foreign Investment in the Forest Sector in the Russian Far East and Potential Market Integration with Northeast Asia." Laxenburg, Austria: IIASA. IIASA Working Paper 94–92.

————. 1994b. "South Korea—Potential Market for Russian Logs." Laxenburg, Austria: IIASA. IIASA Working Paper 94–93.

Williamson, Oliver E. 1975. *Markets and Hierarchies*. New York: Free Press.

————. 1991. "Comparative Economic Organization: The Analysis of Discrete Structural Alternatives." *Administrative Science Quarterly* 36, 2: 269–96.

Wörgötter, Andreas. 1997. "Investment Opportunities in the Russian Regions." Paper presented at the conference "Investing in the Russian Regions," London, 15–16 April 1997.

Zysman, John. 1996. "Reorganizing the European Economy: Production Networks and the Place of Central/Eastern Europe and the Former Soviet Union." Berkeley, Calif. Unpublished manuscript.

PATHS AND PROBLEMS OF THE INTEGRATION OF POST-COMMUNIST RUSSIA INTO THE GLOBAL ECONOMY: A CONCEPT PAPER[1]

Manuel Castells

> After a bitter experience we learned that all-encompassing governmentalization sooner or later will hinder progress.
>
> – Gennadi Zyuganov, in a public speech launching his campaign as presidential candidate of the Russian Communist Party, Moscow, 17 March 1996

INTRODUCTION

The transformation of Russia, and of its geopolitical sphere of influence, to a market economy is a fundamental process that will reshape the European economy, and the global economy as well, in the years to come. Granted, because of the devastating industrial crisis during the transition period, Russia's GDP appears to be only slightly above South Korea's, and because of the rigors of adjustment policies, the impoverishment of the large majority of Russians translates into a very narrow solvent market in the short term. Yet, the preeminent position of Russia in energy, natural resources, rare and precious metals, its scientific potential, its educated population, its unabated geopolitical significance, and the promise of a potential 300-million-person consumer market in the lands of the ex-Soviet Union, still gravitating around Russia, are factors that lead to consideration of the gradual integration of Russia into the global market economy as one of the defining features of the future European economic area. This paper explores the uncertain paths and serious problems faced by this process of integration as of mid-1997. It also reflects on potential assets and strategies to ensure integration in favorable conditions, for both Russia and the rest of Europe. It is a concept paper because while illustrating the analysis with some empirical observations, it does not pretend to provide a quantified assessment of the evolution of the Russian economy in its international environment. My purpose here is to build an argument on the specificity of linkages between Russia and the global economy, relying on trends observed in the 1990s. I will base my analysis on the studies I directed and the field work I conducted in Moscow, Szelenograd, St. Petersburg, Novosibirsk, Tyumen', Nizhnivartovsk, Khabarovsk, and Sakhalin, in several research programs in 1989, 1990, 1991, 1992, 1993, 1995, and 1996.[2] In addition, I will use a number of statistical sources and reports published in Russian newspapers and journals, as well as in the international business press.[3]

THE FALLACIOUS INTERNATIONAL ISOLATION OF THE SOVIET ECONOMY

For geopolitical reasons, the Soviet economy was built on the premise of self-reliance vis-à-vis the international capitalist economies. But over time, this premise was belied by the imperatives of technological dependence, agricultural crisis, and, in the 1980s, the growing demand for consumer goods.[4] In the mid-1970s, the Soviet Union had to resort to massive agricultural imports, particularly of grain, and to high-value imports of advanced machinery and information technology systems in order to keep up with the West in its military-industrial sector. To pay for them, the Soviet Union used its gold reserves, exports of natural resources, rare metals, and diamonds, and, above all, oil and gas exports. In the late 1980s, energy exports accounted for two-thirds of hard currency earnings of the Soviet Union. All together, exports of manufactured goods and services accounted for less than 10 percent of hard currency earnings. In addition, a substantial part of foreign trade (around 25 percent) was conducted through barter, particularly with developing countries and with countries in the Soviet sphere of influence.

Foreign direct investment (FDI) was a negligible factor in the Soviet economy, although it did have some strategic and symbolic importance. Fiat made cars in Togliattigrad, Amper-Uraltel (a Spanish company) made telephones in Perm, and a handful of joint ventures provided a symbolic presence of Western capitalism (usually through politically mediated deals), but by and large foreign investment was not in the picture. So, on the one hand, the Soviet Union was in fact de-linked from the global economy; but, on the other hand, it was dependent on essential imports, and thus its primary commodity exports were in a pattern closer to that of a developing country than to the third largest industrial economy in the world. In fact, the Soviet Union was both at the same time.

Gorbachev's attempt to build a mixed economy, with a politically controlled linkage to the global economy, failed, and this failure triggered a profound crisis that damaged Russia's export capacity, thus depleting its imports as well. The collapse of foreign trade in 1991-93 was followed by a recovery in 1994–96, yet it remained in value below the 1991 level until 1996, for both imports and exports. FDI in 1990–94 posted a modest total between $3 billion and $5 billion, depending on estimates, to be compared with $26 billion in China in 1993 alone. So by the mid-1990s, the Russian economy on the surface appeared to be even less integrated in the system of international exchanges than that of the Soviet Union. Yet the picture is somewhat more complicated (Kur'yerov 1996). First of all, in spite of the shrinkage of foreign trade, the role of the external sector in the Russian economy substantially increased in the 1990s. By the end of 1994, exports represented about 25 percent of Russian GDP, and imports about 17 percent (Kur'yerov 1995a, 1995b), thus making the share of the external sector over GDP twice as high as in the United States. The reason for this apparent paradox is obvious: the Russian economy shrank faster than foreign trade. Thus a smaller external sector has become in fact a more important and most dynamic part of the economy. Second, financial flows are now a critical linkage between Russia and the global economy, and leading Russian companies are in the process of fast internationalization of their shareholdings. Third, FDI was picking up in 1996–97 and seemed to be waitings in the wing for exceptional opportunities, provided that a number of conditions (outlined below) were fulfilled. Fourth, some atypical forms of international business deals, arising from the global criminal economy, seem to have found a land of opportunity in the new Russia. Let us examine these various aspects of economic globalization after briefly surveying the collapse of Russia's industrial structure in the first half of the 1990s.

THE DEINDUSTRIALIZATION OF RUSSIA AND THE COLLAPSE OF HIGH-TECHNOLOGY MANUFACTURING IN THE 1990s

The collapse of Russian industry in the immediate aftermath of the disintegration of the Soviet Union is nothing short of extraordinary. A chart in the appendix displays the decline of industrial output in 1991–94, on the basis of an analysis by the respected economist and academician Valery Kuleshov appears in Kuleshov 1994. The trend has continued at a slower pace in 1994–96. At the heart of the problem are four main issues. The first was the inability, and to some extent unwillingness, of the democratic Russian state to pursue its military buildup. Since the military-industrial complex accounted for at least 50 percent of industrial output, this shrinkage of military outlays simply crippled the core of Russian and Soviet manufacturing. Conversion was attempted, but in the most chaotic form and with little chance to acquire the equipment and know-how that was necessary to open up new production lines. Second, the disintegration of the planned economy before a market could function effectively led to disarticulation of linkages between supply and demand, irreparably damaging the industrial structure, so that an entirely new one had to emerge on the basis of market relationships. The process of privatization that should induce this new market-oriented indutrial sector was, to a large extent, used for the personal benefit of industrial managers and state bureaucrats, who transferred funds abroad to personally controlled accounts and disinvested in the firms. Indeed, they actually benefited from the subsequent social problems that put political pressure on the government to keep subsidies going into noncompetitive firms. Third, adjustment policies and chaotic transitions to the market impoverished the Russian population, reduced living standards to a substantially lower level than that of Soviet times (the good old times of stagnation, as they now say in Russia), thus shrinking solvent demand (Tchernina 1996; Kazantseva and Kuksanova 1997). True, a small urban sector of professionals, businessmen, politicians, and mafiosi (at most between 5 and 10 percent of the population of Moscow and St.Petersburg) has fueled an explosion of conspicuous consumption, but this is essentially a market for expensive imported consumer goods and services. Fourth, as a result of the disorganization of the economy, and of the penetration of administrations by organized crime, the ability of the state to collect taxes from businesses and wealthy individuals simply vanished. In 1996, only one-third of the small proportion of firms that registered to pay taxes did actually pay them on time. Because of this fiscal crisis, the government is increasingly unable to pay wages, pensions, and orders to firms, and since people and companies do not receive payments, they withold their own contributions. Thus, by the end of 1996, total nonpayments in the Russian economy were estimated at about $90 billion, which is about 21 percent of GDP. Without government subsidies or orders, the inefficient state enterprise sector is simply unable to modernize or survive, bringing most of the economy down with its own demise. Russian GDP fell for six straight years in 1991–96. In spite of optimistic Western forecasts during the 1996 presidential elections, GDP declined by an additional 6 percent in 1996.

Perhaps the most lasting industrial catastrophe of the Russian crisis, and one of direct relevance for the research program to which this paper belongs, is the demise of advanced electronics manufacturing. At the root of the problem lies the Soviet backwardness in information technology industries. In the study I directed on microelectronics factories in Zelenograd (the Soviet Silicon Valley, near Moscow) in 1991–93, we could observe a lack of sophistication in products and processes, in spite of the high quality of scientists and engineers (Castells and Natalushko 1994). For instance, integration capacity was, at most, for 3-micron chips, and the "clean rooms" were so dirty that impurities were found in over 30 percent of the chips produced. Soviet computers, according to my interviews in 1990 and 1991 in one of the leading research centers in informatics at the Academy of Sciences Institutes in Akademgorodok, Siberia, were at least ten years behind American computers, in spite of having been at scientific parity in 1960 (Castells and Hall 1994). The reasons for the Soviet lag in information technology lie deep in the structure of the Soviet system but can be summarized under three headings (Castells and Kiselyova 1995): the complete domination of the industry by military requirements, the subsequent isolation of the Soviet industry from technological supplies and exchanges with the rest of the world, and the constraints on diffusion of technological knowledge and information on the civilian industry and on the society at large. The result of this technological backwardness was that when in the 1990s Russian military markets shrank, technological obsolescence prevented Russian microelectronics and computer firms from competing with foreign companies, both abroad and in the domestic market. The value of chip production in Russia declined from $1.5 billion in 1989 to an incredible $385 million in 1995. The advanced segments of the industry were devastated: out of 140 microelectronics manufacturers existing in 1990, by 1995, 130 had closed down. For the remaining 10 firms, manufacturing costs increased by 4,000 percent. These companies, and several telecommunications equipment producers, were barely surviving in the mid-1990s as subcontractors for low-technology Asian companies, producing toys and digital watches. When in 1996 I again interviewed engineers of the leading microlectronics company that I had studied in Zelenograd in 1992, they reported that 50 percent of their factory was producing shampoo [*sic*] for the Russian market. The most technologically advanced company still in the microelectronics business in Zelenograd, Mikron, became a joint venture with Hua Ko Electronics, a Hong Kong firm that bought 50 percent of Mikron's shares for $18 million. Indeed, the most profitable business in Zelenograd became the sale of assets and shares to foreign investors. But there were few takers. An example will explain why: the rise and fall of an IBM PC computer factory in Zelenograd. In 1993 IBM linked up with Kvant, a former military electronics enterprise, to produce 40,000 PCs per month for the Russian market, by an agreement with the Russian government, under which IBM-Kvant would be exempted from taxes on imported components. This was essential, precisely because there was no reliable supplier of components in Russia. It was a commercial success. In 1995, Russians bought about one million PCs, 40 percent of which were supplied by IBM. IBM-Kvant employed 1,000 workers, and the value of its output was estimated at around $960 million per year. Then in 1994, the Russian parliament approved a law eliminating the tax exemption on imported components (for a value of about 8.5 percent of the cost of finished product). This put IBM at a competitive disadvantage with the Russian trading companies that were importing finished PCs (mainly from China and Southeast Asia) and that continued to be tax exempt. That was precisely the intention of the law since the powerful lobby of import/export companies had its way in the Duma. On 27 February 1996, IBM stopped assembling PCs in Zelenograd. Most workers became idle again, as the plant was reconverted into a repair and maintenance shop for IBM PCs imported into Russia. For all practical purposes, PC production stopped.

Without access to technology, equipment, supplies, and know-how, the Russian electronics industry became a low-level subsidiary of low-level Asian producers, with the exception of a small number of firms that continued to work for the defense ministry on the basis of imported components and foreign technology (either licensed or copied through reverse engineering).

The consequences of this collapse of the civilian microelectronics/computer/telecommunications industries for the new Russia are far-reaching. First, they make the new Russian economy entirely dependent on imports for its advanced technological infrastructure. Second, they eliminate the possibility of industrial know-how that could make possible the existence of Russian firms as part of an electronic producers' network. This does not preclude the possibility of foreign electronics implants in Russia, but they would have to operate largely in isolation from the Russian industrial environment, which limits the possibility and the interest of these producer networks in Russia. Third, the complete dependence of Russia, still a nuclear superpower, on foreign supplies/know-how in advanced electronics and communication technology cripples its capacity for again becoming a credible, autonomous military power in conventional warfare, except for the unthinkable option of blowing up the planet.

A similar story can be told about the strategic energy industry, with the partial exception of the relatively well-managed gas industry, controlled by the giant corporation Gazprom (Kiselyova, Castells, and Granberg 1996). Oil production dropped by 40 percent between 1987 and 1996. In 1996, investment in the gas industry fell by 5.5 percent and in the oil industry by 25.7 percent. Even profitable oil companies, such as Yukos and Sidanko, halved their investment in 1996. Overall, manufacturing investment in 1996 fell by 16 percent in comparison to 1995, reaching an all-time low level at slightly over $18 billion. This, in spite of the rosy forecasts about economic recovery in 1996, after the artificial stimulus during the presidential elections campaign, and the relative stability brought by the political defeat of Communists in the 1996 presidential elections. Thus, in the aftermath of the demise of the Soviet Union, the world's third largest industrial power has become the world's largest industrial wreckage.

THE LIMITS OF INTERNATIONAL TRADE AND FDI

Russia's external trade recovered somewhat in the 1994–96 period, after a dramatic decline that found its lowest point in 1993. In 1996, for the first time it recovered its level of 1990 in terms of value, with total turnover trade evaluated at $141.7 billion in 1997 prices, up 4 percent of the 1995 figure. Exports increased to $87.7 billion, and imports to $59.7 billion, thus posting a positive trade balance, mainly due to the relatively low import capacity of the country. In 1996, trade with Commonwealth of Independent States (CIS) countries was the fastest growing segment of foreign trade, and Ukraine became the most important Russian trade partner, reflecting the low competitiveness of Russia with the rest of the world. Besides Ukraine, Russia's main partners, in rank order, are Germany, China, and the United States.

The structure of both exports and imports seems rather stable. From the last reliable data, for 1995, it can be observed that exports are still concentrated in the fuel and energy sector (accounting for about 50 percent of total exports), natural resources, and raw materials. The share of machinery and equipment in exports continues to hover at around a low 5 percent of the total. On the other hand, about 30 percent of imports is accounted for by machinery, and another one-third by food. Overall, the structure of trade reflects the persistence of an economy of survival, depleting natural and energy resources for export and using the earnings for buying food, essential machinery and equipment items, and, lately, specialty consumer goods. This structure has a weak link: the crisis of the oil industry. In a study of Siberian oil and gas, Kiselyova, Castells, and Granberg (1996) showed the structural and political sources of accelerated obsolescence of the oil industry, depletion of the fields, and crisis of management. Furthermore, to the problems of oil production must be added the problems of transportation, as the state-owned pipeline operator Transneft is becoming unable to ensure the reliable operation of the pipelines. This limitation and the shrinking access to ports limit oil companies to exporting only 2 million barrels a day, about one-third of Russian production. Although gas exports are more stable, by themselves they cannot provide the necessary hard currency to pay for imports necessary for the modernization of the Russian economy. Thus, the positive balance of Russian trade is a mirage: it results from an inability to import rather than from the performance of exports. It reflects, in fact, the dwindling capacity of Russia to participate in foreign trade because of its declining export base vis-à-vis its import needs. Unless the energy sector recovers through a major technological and industrial overhauling, Russia will become increasingly marginalized from international trade. The main loser in this process, besides Russia itself, will be the European Union, which in 1996 accounted for about 40 percent of Russia's foreign trade, and which is obviously positioned to be the privileged partner of a dynamic, modernized Russian economy—if such an economy were to exist in the future.

Can FDI be the answer to the needs of modernization that cannot be met by foreign trade? I doubt it, in spite of recent growth of foreign investment in 1996 and early 1997. Let us examine the data and illustrate the issue with our observation on FDI in the new oil and gas fields off Sakhalin Island.

According to Russian government data in January 1997, total foreign investment in Russia in 1991–96 reached a cumulative total of $12 billion. This compares unfavorably with the approximate $25 billion *per year, on average,* received by China during the same period. Furthermore, half of this total was invested in 1996, prompting Prime Minister Viktor Chernomyrdin's optimism that Russia was now on its way to attracting investment, but also underscoring its dismal performance for most of the 1990s. Other sources, however, challenge these estimates and put the actual volume of FDI for 1996 at just $1.2 billion.

However, even more troubling than the low volume of foreign investment is the character of this investment, essentially concentrated in buying assets, or stocks, at a bargain price, hoping for their future revaluation. A survey of foreign investors conducted in 1996 showed that their preferences for investment were concentrated in three sectors: telecommunications, energy, and oil, followed at some distance by forestry, banking, and metallurgy.[5] Indeed, even in the current situation of negative economic growth, in 1992–95 the foreign acquired assets were revalued three- to tenfold (Denisova 1995). A case in point is Gazprom, the giant state-controlled gas consortium, managing about 40 percent of the world's natural gas reserves. In 1994 the stock market valued its reserves at three-tenths of $1 per barrel of oil equivalent, compared to $10.3 for British Gas. Whoever bought its shares is sure to make a hefty profit in not such a long time. Thus, most of this portfolio investment aims more at financial gains than at reconstructing the Russian economy. Russian interests, and particularly company managers and government apparatchiki who presided over the privatization process, kept the most valuable property under their control, yet devalued stocks of privatized companies in order to offer substantial profits to foreign partners in exchange for instant cash, most often kept in bank accounts abroad.

FDI in production is proceeding with extraordinary precautions in the situation of legal uncertainty, bureaucratic arbitrariness, and safety concerns that characterize Russia's wild capitalism. Even in the profitable oil and gas sector, prudence is the rule. Our research on investment by American and Japanese companies in the most promising offshore oil and gas drilling on Sakhalin shows that, while substantial investment could come from these companies (about $25 billion in twenty years—twice as much as cumulative foreign investment in post-Communist Russia until now), firm commitments await the final passage of special legislation that would guarantee entire freedom of movement for capital and management of production to foreign companies. The Law on Production Sharing Agreements was finally passed by the Duma in 1996, but its decrees of application are so slow to come and so contradictory that in early 1997 the overall legislative and administrative environment remained confused, thus discouraging firm commitments from foreign companies and limiting their activity to preliminary operations. Sakhalin I Project (formed by Exxon, SODECO [Japan National Oil Co.], and the Russian companies Rosneft and Sakhalinmorneftegaz) was planning to continue surveys in the summer of 1997 to confirm reserves. Sakhalin II (including Marathon Oil, McDermott, Shell, Mitsui, and Mitsubishi) was installing mobile drilling in Molikpaq in the spring of 1997. U.S. vice-president Al Gore and Prime Minister Chernomyrdin, in a meeting on 7 February 1997, emphasized the priority given by the two countries to successful cooperation in energy development on Sakhalin. In February 1997, ABN-AMRO, a Dutch bank, and Lazard Frères gave conditional approval to $13 billion in credit to the Russian companies Rosneft and Sakhalinmorneftegaz to finance the development of oil fields in the Okhotsk Sea, in the framework of the Sakhalin I Project. However, a credit line of only $10 million was operational, until an agreement could be reached on a safe and effective route for the transportation of extracted oil. Thus, business projects are moving along on Sakhalin, but at a slow pace, until institutional and infrastructural conditions are fulfilled. To legal uncertainty must be added the rift between the Moscow and Sakhalin governments concerning Sakhalin's future riches. In February 1997 the Sakhalin Duma passed a resolution halting the transfer of all payments to the federal treasury because of nonpayment of wages owed to Sakhalin workers by the Ministry of Finance. The net result of uncertainty and conflicts is that while there is an extroardinary potential for oil and gas fields ready for exploitation 40 kilometers away from the coast of energy-hungry Japan, the economic situation on the island is critical, and people, free to move, are leaving the island in great numbers. A report in the *Russian Far East News* of March 1997 reads

> Sakhalin is not the easiest place to live and do business. Food prices are currently rising and selection is going down. Tax and custom authorities are getting more aggressive in collecting money. Energy problems on Sakhalin are also worse now and blackouts are common. The general business climate is more difficult than even two years ago (p. 9).

In 1995 in Yuzhno-Sakhalinsk, federal government representatives were telling us of the future of Sakhalin as the "Kuwait of the Pacific." But common people with whom we met replied: "We do not really believe [in] a rich future, but if it happens, it will not be for us. Bureaucrats will take it all for themselves." This anecdote has an analytical meaning that will become evident in the conclusion to this paper.

As for the huge gas reserves and still important oil fields in Western Siberia, they appear to offer little attraction to foreign investment because of the need to rely on unpredictable government controls for production and transportation and because of obscure conditions under which deals are made in the industry. In other words, foreign capital, for understandable reasons, aims at taking advantage of Russia's energy and natural resources while being as little involved as possible in the Russian economy and setting up its own operating structure, in a pattern typical of Western investment in developing countries in earlier times. At the same time, the Russian government and Russian companies' strategy seems to be to attract foreign capital to prepackaged deals, without relinquishing control, except when there is no alternative (for example, a lack of technology and equipment for offshore drilling). The consequence of these conflicting strategies is the slowing down of the international connection of Russia's energy sector, in spite of its obvious potential for both Russia and global energy supply.

THE GLOBALIZATION OF RUSSIAN FINANCE AND STOCK MARKETS

The bright spot of the Russian economy in 1996–97 was the flow of global capital into emerging Russian stock markets. In the wake of the success of Russia's Eurobond offer of $1 billion in 1996, the Moscow stock market increased its value by 127 percent in 1996 and by an additional 65 percent in the first three months of 1997.

Foreign investment in Russian government short-term securities (GKOs) reached $6.7 billion by February 1997. In the first three months of 1997 global investors (many of them mutual funds and securities companies from around the world) invested $1.2 billion in Russian stocks. The reason for this rush is obvious: Russia is the cheapest emerging market. Risks are high, but payoffs are potentially substantial. With Yeltsin recovering from his ailments, for the time being, and a new team of capable reformers, led by Chubais and Nemtsov at the helm of economic policy, with full presidential backing, investors scanning the world for opportunities in emerging markets are willing to bet a small fraction of their capital in what could be a most profitable market if even a small segment of the Russian economy stabilizes and grows in the medium term. Thus, the price-earnings ratios of leading Russian stocks, such as Lukoil or telecommunication companies, are double or triple that of their foreign equivalents. Granted, this economic revival is affecting a tiny proportion of the Russian population, mainly concentrated in the middle class sectors of Moscow and St. Petersburg, and by and large excluding the non-European areas of Russia. Investor interest is usually limited to utilities and energy companies, but this is a large enough sector to ensure a segmented integration of Russia in the global economy. It could be a beginning. However, the problem is that a substantial proportion of these profits is not reinvested in Russia, so that the process is not self-sustaining. Much global investment aims at speculating on short-term profits and dumping the stocks before excessive risks take over the promise. Thus, while Russia's financial markets were experiencing an unusual bonanza in 1997, prompting Chernomyrdin to forecast $20 billion in foreign investment in the year 2000, the slightest hint of an institutional crisis would lead to a financial crash, as nervous global investors are on the alert to avoid losses. Indeed, the globalization of Russian finance is a two-way process, and the main direction is outward from Russia. According to a report in *Izvestiia* (18 February 1997), capital flight from Russia for the last five years is estimated at about $60 billion, with most of the money being deposited in bank accounts in Switzerland and other locations, such as Cyprus. Brokers and securities firms are the thriving sector of Moscow's economy, and financial giants, such as Menatep, control large sectors of the otherwise crumbling Russian economy. The only truly dynamic integration of Russia into the global economy is conducted through the intermediation between global investors, devalued Russian assets, and the recycling of profits in international financial markets and foreign bank accounts. And this process is largely connected to Russia's shadow economy, which conditions and shapes Russian's linkage to the European economy.

THE INTERNATIONAL IMPLICATIONS OF RUSSIA'S SHADOW ECONOMY

It has become commonplace to emphasize the widespread penetration of Russian business and government agencies by illegal, and sometimes criminal, networks. Unfortunately, it is indeed a fundamental issue. A 1994 report on organized crime by the Analytical Center for Social and Economic Policies of the Presidency of Russia estimated that pratically all small private firms were paying tribute to criminal groups. As for the larger private firms and commercial banks, it was reported that between 70 and 80 percent were paying protection dues to criminal groups. These payments represented between 10 and 20 percent of capital turnover for these firms, an amount equivalent to over half of their profits (reported by *Izvestiia*, 26 January 1994). The situation does not seem to have improved much in 1997. According to a more recent *Izvestiia* report (18 February 1997), it is estimated that about 41,000 industrial companies, 50 percent of banks, and 80 percent of joint ventures have criminal connections. The shadow economy, in all its manifestations, may account for as much as 40 percent of Russia's economy. The collapse of the taxation system is directly related to the payment by business to extortion organizations to solve their problems, in the absence of a reliable state. Faced with a choice between an unresponsive administration and an effective, if ruthless, racketeering business, firms and individuals are growing accustomed to relying on the second, out of fear or convenience or both.

The expansion of illegal business and criminal organizations in Russia is a direct consequence of the lack of political control that characterized the transition from statism to unfettered capitalism. As distinguished economist and Sovietologist Marshall Goldman wrote:

> The breakup of the Soviet Union was accompanied by the collapse of the economic infrastructure; Gosplan, the ministries, the wholesale operations—all simply disappeared. Eventually, there was an institutional vacuum. On top of everything else, there was no accepted code of business behavior. Suddenly Russia found itself with the makings of a market but with no commercial code, no effective bank system, no effective accounting system, no procedures for declaring bankruptcy. What was left over was not

> very helpful, especially the prevaling notion that it was perfectly appropriate to cheat the state (1996: 44).

Without institutions and laws, and with the old nomenklatura and many of the new politicos riding the wave of privatization for their own sake, criminal networks proliferated in the interstices of a crumbling system and ensured the linkage between all kinds of supplies and all kinds of demands—for a price. Although the situation seemed to be settling down in 1997, in part because the most prominent ringleaders had become respectable global capitalists, the impact of the criminalization of large segments of economic activity will be a lasting one—among other reasons, because solid linkages have been established between the various Russian mafias and criminal organizations around the world, giving a new impulse to the formation of an interconnected global criminal economy (Hadelman 1995; Sterling 1994; Castells 1998). Moreover, without safe and reliable conditions for investment in Russia, foreign investors can only venture under the protection of powerful groups in the government or in the crime-penetrated business world. This is why stock acquisitions in the financial markets are the safest bet, in spite of the obvious risks. They do not require daily managing of investments in Russia, except for small outfits run by frontier financial managers. A significant proportion of exports in oil, precious stones, metals, and natural resources is smuggled, attracting into these deals the most venturesome fringe of international business. Indeed, the Baltic republics are among the world's largest exporters of some minerals that they do not produce and hardly import.

Perhaps the most damaging dimension of the pervasiveness of Russia's shadow economy, with its criminal underpinnings, is the destruction of trust among the Russian population at large. Trust is the foundation of investment, thus of growth, thus of market expansion, thus of opening opportunities for global trade, investment, and production networks. This trust has disappeared in Russia. As a respected journalist, Pavel Voshchanov, wrote,

> Where does the mafia take its source from? This is simple; it begins with the common interests of politicians, business people, and gangsters. All others are hostages of this unholy alliance—all others mean us (1995).

CONCLUSION: THE REAL PROSPECTS FOR THE INTEGRATION OF RUSSIA IN THE EUROPEAN ECONOMY

The logic presented in this paper, on the basis of observations, facts, and trends during the 1990s, leads to a dead end for the integration of Russia in the global economy, thus in the European economy. Under current parameters it would probably be limited to the globalization of finance, to dwindling exports of energy and natural resources in exchange for imports shrinking at an even faster pace, and to the acquisition of stocks and devalued assets by foreign investors at a bargain price and with a primarily speculative focus. This evolution would be socially, thus politically, untenable. A humiliated, impoverished, abused Russia would turn to radical nationalism, breaking up its weak international ties and rebuilding, once again, a military power to be feared—starting with a technological overhaul of the armed forces. It may be Lebed, it may be someone else (not Zhirinovsky, who is probably a puppet of the KGB, and not the Communists, whose past makes them ineligible for the younger segment of the electorate). But if Russia does not make gradual steps of improvement in connection with the European economy, it will eventually rebuild a state to challenge this economy from the outside.

So what are the prospects for a different scenario, one that would rebuild the Russian economy as a market economy, bringing it in close connection with the European Union, for their mutual benefit? In a nutshell: the Russian economy has to be rebuilt from within. There is capital; there is skilled labor; there is still, but not for long, infrastucture; there is an abundance of energy and natural resources; there is managerial and scientific capacity; there is some entrepreneurial spirit (Khotin 1996); and there is, potentially, a large market, which should include not only the 148 million Russians, but also the other 143 million people from the ex-Soviet Union, whose economy is in fact entirely dependent on Russia's evolution. But how to start a process that would eventually reverse the current downward trend? As all development processes start: with investment. There is indeed an abundance of capital in Russia that chooses not to invest in Russia. As I mentioned above, it is estimated that in the last five years capital flight from Russia amounted to about $60 billion. This does not include foreign accounts legally held by Russian companies for their international operations. But there is more. It is estimated that Russian households, rightly distrustful of banks and of the fate of the ruble, keep $30 billion in cash, usually under their beds. This is six times the amount of total foreign investment in 1991–96. Whatever is saved is saved in dollar bills, for an emergency.[6] The mobilization of these savings, as well as the opening of opportunities for investment of current capital flight, would make available tens of billions of dollars for investment in Russia. Granted, the development of a technological and communication infrastructure and the existence of an appropriate legal environment, including tax reform and accounting procedures and a reliable financial system, are prerequisites for investment to proceed productively. Both foreign aid and government policy should concentrate on building this infrastructure and on consolidating institutions once basic macroeconomic parameters seem to have been stabilized. Yet unless trust is restored/created for both households and firms, there will be little domestic investment in Russia, and the market will not expand. The combination of semilegal global finance and the shadow economy would then continue to dominate the Russian economic scene.

How to restore trust? At the heart of the problem is the correct perception of widespread linkages among politics, business, and crime, together with a deep-seated distrust of the government. Thus, the most important step is to sever the links between government (and politics) and business—to set private business free and to concentrate government efforts on protecting business against the mafias. If a number of symbolic episodes show a new determination toward the rule of law, if political leaders stop embezzling funds and trafficking influence, and if in people's experience business becomes a reliable activity, in a few years, some level of trust could be established and investment could be mobilized. Then Russia could start growing, offering its most important asset to the European economy: a significant market, not only through imports, but also through reverse production networks: European companies producing in Russia, at lower cost, for the Russian market. Once Russia modernizes and becomes a dynamic, competitive economy, then its incorporation into the European Union's sphere of economic influence could set the conditions for a multilayered networking of economic activities.

Is this feasible? It basically depends on political conditions. But time and patience are running out. The new Russian government appointed by Yeltsin in 1997 gave hopeful signals in its first steps. The stated attempt to free the Russian economy from the giant state-backed monopolies that absorb resources and international linkages for the benefit of the new nomenklatura is a most significant test. Nemtsov declared his intention to ensure free competition for all firms in government tenders. The resignation of Radionov, the minister of energy, in April 1997 was a sign that something may be changing in the decisive energy sector. Chubais and Nemtsov have a difficult task in front of them. Their only chance to succeed in the reform with which Gaidar failed (under more difficult conditions, it is true) is to act quickly in breaking the hold of government, big business, and criminal networks on Russian investors, workers, and consumers. Should they make some progress in the right direction and should their successors decide to serve Russia rather than to serve themselves, a new Russian economy could still emerge at the turn of the millennium—and with it, a new peaceful, stable, and prosperous Europe.

This paper was written in May 1997.

NOTES

1. Prepared for the Bruno Kreisky Forum for International Dialogue, in the framework of the BRIE-Kreisky Project on Foreign Direct Investment and Trade in Eastern and Central Europe.
2. These studies were conducted in cooperation with the Institute of Economics and Industrial Engineering of the Soviet (then Russian) Academy of Sciences, Siberian Branch; with the Russian Sociological Association; and with the Institute of Youth, Center for Advanced Sociology, in Moscow. They were sponsored by various institutions: the Spanish government's Center for Sociological Research, the Spanish Electronics Industry Association, and the University of California's Pacific Rim Program. For findings of these studies, I refer to research reports and publications cited below.
3. I have used a variety of sources from the Russian press and economic journals, from the international business press, and from the daily digest of the Russian press reported on-line by the Open Media Research Institute.

Russian sources have been collected and analyzed by Emma Kiselyova, Research Associate, University of California at Berkeley. For the sake of simplicity in this paper I have not considered necessary to give a specific source for each one of the data cited since these are facts widely reported in the press. I have, however, provided a specific source for observations that seem to be critical, as well as for academic sources.

4. References and data concerning the Soviet economy up to 1991, particularly the characteristics of Soviet technology, are reported in Castells and Kiselyova (1995). This note should be considered as a generic call to sources included in this book. For an insightful analysis of the issues raised by the post-Soviet economic transition, see Cohen and Schwartz (1993). For a more orthodox account on the matter, see Aslund (1995).
5. ICR Survey Group; reported in "Zapadny'ye portfel'ny'ye investitsii v Rossiyu," *EKO*, no. 10 (1996): 117–23.
6. The estimate of $30 billion is reported by *Business Week*, 24 March 1997. As a striking illustration of the preference of Russian housholds for cash hard currency over financial assets, see the recent study on the evolution of expenses in the budget of households in Novosibirsk *oblast* in Kazantseva and Kuksanova (1997).

REFERENCES

Aslund, Anders. 1995. *How Russia Became a Market Economy*. Washington, D.C.: Brookings Institution.

Castells, Manuel. 1998. *The Information Age: Economy, Society and Culture*. Volume 3, *End of Millennium*. Oxford: Blackwell.

Castells, Manuel, and Emma Kiselyova. 1995. *The Collapse of the Soviet Union: The View from the Information Society*. Berkeley: International and Area Studies.

Castells, Manuel, and Svetlana Natalushko. 1994. *La Modernización tecnológica de las empresas de electrónica y telecomunicaciones en Rusia: Un Estudio de Zelenograd*. Madrid: Universidad Autonoma de Madrid, Programa de Estudios Rusos. Research Monograph.

Cohen, Stephen, and Andrew Schwartz. 1993. "Privatization in the Former Soviet Empire: The Tunnel at the End of the Light." *American Prospect*, no. 13: 99–108.

Denisova, I. I. 1995. "Fondovyi rynok i inostrannye investitsii." *EKO*, no. 4: 65–73.

Goldman, Marshall I. 1996. "Why Is the Mafia so Dominant in Russia?" *Challenge*, January/February, pp. 39–47.

Handelman, Stephen. 1995. *Comrade Criminal: Russia's New Mafiya.* New Haven: Yale University Press.

Kazantseva, L. K., and N. V. Kuksanova. 1997. "Sotsial'naya tsena reform." *EKO,* no. 2: 128–41.

Khotin, Leonid. 1996. "Old and New Entrepreneurs in Today's Russia." *Problems of Postcommunism,* January/February, pp. 49–57.

Kiselyova, Emma; Manuel Castells; and Alexander Granberg. 1996. *The Missing Link: Siberian Oil and Gas and the Pacific Economy.* Berkeley: Institute of Urban and Regional Development. Research Monograph.

Kuleshov, Valery I. 1994. "Perekhodnaya economika: Proidennye etapy, nametivshiyeysa tendentsii." *EKO,* no. 1: 53–62.

Kur'yerov, V. G. 1995a. "Vneshneekonomicheskiye svyazi." *EKO,* no. 3: 77–98.

————. 1995b. "Vneshneekonomicheskiye svyazi." *EKO,* no. 9: 51–75.

————. 1996. "Vneshneekonomicheskiye svyazi." *EKO,* no. 10: 58–75.

Sterling, Claire. 1994. *Thieves' World: The Threat of the New Global Nnetwork of Organized Crime.* New York: Simon and Schuster.

Tchernina, Natalia. 1996. *Economic Transition and Social Exclusion in Russia.* Geneva: International Institute for Labour Studies. Research Series.

Voshchanov, Pavel. 1995. "Mafia Godfathers Become Fathers of the Nation." *Konsomolskaya Pravda,* May; cited from the English version in *Business World of Russia Weekly,* 15 May, pp. 13–14.

THE ROOTS OF AND REMEDIES FOR RUSSIA'S RACKET ECONOMY

M. Steven Fish

> Our political malaise is due to the same cause as our social malaise: that is, to the lack of secondary cadres to interpose between the individual and the State. We have seen that these secondary groups are essential if the State is not to oppress the individual: they are also necessary if the State is to be sufficiently free of the individual.
>
> – Emile Durkheim[1]

> No law is worthy of the name unless applied by a sovereign.
>
> – Theodore Lowi[2]

This essay considers the causes of and possible remedies for the emergence of a "racket economy" in post-Soviet Russia.[3] The racket economy differs from the Soviet-era command economy insofar as the former is not fully statized. But in a racket economy there nevertheless exist intimate proximity of public and private power; oligarchic, market-constricting control over the economy's commanding heights; nearly complete corruption of officialdom responsible for economic policy; and the absence of any semblance of the rule of law in the realm of economic activity. What is here called a racket economy may also be conceived of as a "criminalized" or "mafiaized" economy.

Russia's racket economy is the product of the confluence of five factors. None of these is unique to Russia. Each is found in some other countries in the post-Communist world (and elsewhere) as well. The combination of all five causal factors, however, is unusual in comparative perspective. Their joint operation helps account for the distinctive character of the Russian economy. These factors underlie the nonemergence—or, at best, halting and extremely tenuous development—of functioning, market-nurturing institutions. Their continued presence guarantees chronic economic instability, anemic economic performance, and a pattern of national integration into the global economy that benefits only a small portion of the Russian population.

The following section explores the causes of the racket economy and explicates the links between these causes and specific outcomes that have led the Russian economy to the state in which it finds itself over a half dozen years after the collapse of the Soviet regime. Given the elusiveness of the racket economy and the difficulty of accounting for its emergence, no attempt will be made to order or assign relative weights to the causal factors. This paper represents not a truly "finished" explanation for a complicated and poorly understood phenomenon, but rather an early attempt to make some rudimentary sense of it. The second major section of the paper proposes and discusses prescriptions for mitigating the pathologies that jointly have given rise to the racket economy and guaranteed its persistence.

THE ROOTS OF THE RACKET

THE CURSE OF PLENTY

The first factor that has promoted the growth of a racket economy in Russia is the supremacy of raw materials and extractive industries. The dominant position of these sectors to some extent stems from Russia's voluptuous natural endowments in precious metals, gems, oil, and natural gas. It is also a legacy of the economic course pursued by the Communist regime, which relied heavily on the export of these resources to generate foreign exchange while pursuing policies that both decimated agriculture and precluded a shift from extensive to intensive production techniques in industry. Particularly during the late Soviet (post-Khrushchev) period, Russia's rich endowments of raw materials, combined with the absence of a market economy and the country's international economic isolation, allowed for an economics of indolence. It enabled leaders to ignore the need for restructuring and modernization and induced a self-inflicted and crippling dependence on the proceeds from raw materials production and export.

Thus, in the immediate post-Soviet situation, the only industries that were internationally competitive were found in the energy, precious metals, and minerals sectors. This circumstance conduced a rent-seeking approach to economic policy and activity and the emergence of a competitive political game that revolved around gaining access to the proceeds of sales of natural resources. This situation is scarcely unique to Russia. As a large body of literature attests, it is common in countries rich in natural resources, including Nigeria, Zaire, Venezuela, and Indonesia.[4]

THE TRAJECTORY OF ECONOMIC REFORM AND THE PRIVATIZATION OF PUBLIC POLICY

The second cause of the racket is found in the type of economic reform pursued during the first half-decade of the post-Soviet period. Given the bewildering complexity of economic change in Russia, briefly characterizing the trajectory and nature of economic reform is hazardous and difficult. In broadest terms, however, two sets of reforms were particularly crucial. The first was the destruction of the Soviet-era economic policy decision-making system by President Boris Yeltsin and his team of liberal economists, led by Egor Gaidar, in 1992. The second was the implementation of the program of voucher and "loans-for-shares" privatization that followed in 1992–96. The first reform amounted to reorganizing the entire system of economic administration. It involved such measures as enhancing the status of the Finance Ministry, abolishing the Ministry of Industry, and aggressively pursuing policies that severed Soviet-era ties among enterprises and between enterprises and their former creditors. These policies of "creative destruction" quickly launched Russia on a completely different trajectory of reform than that pursued in countries where Soviet-era structures in economic policymaking were left largely intact after the collapse of communism, such as Ukraine and Bulgaria. The first phase of the second crucial reform, privatization, centered on distribution of low-value vouchers to all citizens. Most recipients quickly sold their vouchers to fledgling investors or to the managers of the enterprises in which they were employed. Unlike some other voucher programs, such as that carried out in Czechoslovakia, the Russian program in practice greatly favored sitting enterprise administrators, many of whom promptly gained controlling interest in the firms that they theretofore had managed but not owned. The program set in motion what quickly came to be known in Russia as "nomenklatura privatization," though voucher privatization in itself did not actually create the peculiar form of oligarchy that came to characterize the structure of the Russian economy. That structure resulted largely from the second major phase of privatization, which adopted a loans-for-shares approach, under which the government sold stakes in many of the country's largest firms, including oil and other highly valuable companies, for a tiny fraction of their real worth to a clutch of private banks. Many of these banks had been created during the first phase of reform by the newly privatized enterprises as magnets for attracting low-interest loans from the state and/or as organizations for engaging in currency speculation. Some had already become highly effective rent-seeking machines; the loans-for-shares scheme then catapulted them to control over the economy's commanding heights. The privatization program thus created a private sector dominated by an oligarchy of "financial-industrial groups" (FIGs), most of which encompassed a large bank and a set of enterprises, often quite diversified, controlled by that bank. By the end of 1996, the FIGs in some respects bore a striking resemblance to the prewar Japanese *zaibatsu* or the postwar Korean *chaebol*. Some Russian political and business leaders, moreover, actually characterized these new structures in such terms. They self-consciously fostered their creation and development and claimed that they, like their East Asian counterparts in earlier decades, were the best hope for leading the economy into a new era of prosperity.[5]

Whether or not an economy based on such foundations provides an ideal—or even a viable—basis for economic dynamism in Russia will not be known for some time and must be left to question. The new system certainly differs starkly from the Soviet-era command economy. As one Russian scholar has rightly noted, the new "oligarchic form of coordination can be perceived as the first step away from the Soviet-era system of bureaucratic accommodation, because the pluralism of this [new] oligarchy is rooted in the economy, rather than in government administration."[6] The zaibatsu (and their postwar successors, the *keiretsu*) and the chaebol created workable structures for Japan's and Korea's economic successes, though it is doubtful that their dominance continues to contribute to economic dynamism under conditions prevailing at the end of the twentieth century. What is clear, however, and of most significance for the present paper, is that such oligopolistic concentration of wealth engenders the corruption of the political class, the fusion of political and economic power, and a blurring of the public-private distinction in the economy. Politicians become addicted to the support of one or several of a highly limited number of fonts of wealth, while the survival and prosperity of the conglomerates themselves depend to a great extent on government favors. If such conditions obtained in Japan and Korea, they rapidly developed in Russia to an even higher degree, all the more so given the dominance of extractive industries and raw materials in the Russian case. In Russia, moreover, the desperate state of the state (that is, of the governing administrative apparatus), combined with the enfeeblement of the president, has placed the state itself at a disadvantage vis-à-vis the FIGs. Consequently, the FIGs managed to penetrate the state administration at the highest levels, with figures such as Sibneft's Boris Berezovskii and Oneksimbank's Vladimir Potanin actually assuming ministerial portfolios and other positions in the president's inner circle—without relinquishing de facto control over their respective FIGs. High offices in the state administration, rather than acting as neutral brokers among FIGs, sometimes literally serve as the battleground—and the place of truce-making—among competing oligarchs.[7] Under such conditions, the formation of what would be recognized in the West as genuine business associations is simply unnecessary from the standpoint of the business interests concerned. Some business associations, such as the Association of Russian Banks, the Association of Private and Privatized Enterprises, the Chamber of Commerce and Industry, and the Round Table of Russian Business, have indeed formed during the past several years in Russia. Most are loose agglomerations of FIGs. The real players in the business of shaping pubic policy, however, are the individual FIGs; they are the networks that run Russian politics. The business associations that the FIGs sometimes form and join usually limit themselves to issuing public statements, including and especially declarations concerning their members' importance in the new Russian economy and/or complaints about how this or that sector or group of industries is disadvantaged by foreign competition or by some set of regulations.[8]

The capture of the state apparatus by the captains of the FIGs obscures the distinction between public and private and corrupts the political system. These outcomes also have "second order effects" that are beyond the scope of this paper but that are worthy of note. They include immense—and from the standpoint of sound fiscal policy, utterly unaffordable—tax breaks and other privileges for the concerns controlled by oligarchs who occupy the upper reaches of government or who enjoy close personal connections with those who do.[9] In Russia such a situation by 1997 drove the national government's tax revenues down to a paltry 40 percent of "anticipated" revenue, and tax revenue as a percentage of GDP to a level less than one-third that of Poland or the Czech Republic.

In his acute essay on power written on the eve of World War II, Bertrand Russell noted:

> In every developed country, the bulk of economic power belongs to a small body of individuals. Sometimes these men are private capitalists, as in America, France, and Great Britain; sometimes they are politicians, as in Germany, Italy, and Russia. The latter system arises where economic and political power have coalesced.[10]

Russell's statement serves as a reminder that oligopoly is the rule in advanced industrialized economies. What Russell did not discuss or theorize, however, was the emergence of a form of oligopoly in which the capitalists and the politicians were precisely the same people. Such a system represents a degree of "coalescence" that goes beyond what Russell observed, at least in what he referred to as "developed countries" (which included Russia). It is not unknown in some countries in the contemporary Third World, where sultans and their cronies own most or much of the countries they rule. It is unusual in advanced industrialized countries, however, and sets Russia apart within that group. Russia's oligopoly is also unusual insofar as its constituent parts, unlike those of, say, the Duvalier (Haiti), Somoza (Nicaragua), and Suharto (Indonesia) oligarchies, are not based primarily on familial relations. In fact, the ties that bind the constituent parts of many of the FIGs together are no older than the post-Soviet period itself.

ONE-DIMENSIONAL LIBERALISM, OR "A SAVAGE AND LAWLESS FREEDOM"

The third factor contributing to the emergence of the racket economy was the decision taken by Russia's liberal leaders at the time of the birth of the post-Communist regime to withdraw the state from the business of law enforcement. Tragically, leaders such as Gaidar, Viktor Sheinis, Grigorii Iavlinskii, and many other liberals who influenced the structure and ethos of the new Russian state, ignored the necessity for a strong law-enforcement apparatus. They made precious little distinction between functions and agencies intended for political repression and control and those designed to contain violence, maintain public order, and enforce contracts. They embraced Kant's belief that "there can be no wealth producing activity without freedom" but ignored his injunctions that meaningful freedom implies "renounc[ing] savage and lawless freedom" and embracing "public coercive laws" backed by the full force of state power.[11] Their policies inadvertently created a climate of what Russians call *beznakazannost'*. The word, which may be translated as "impunity" but which actually carries an even stronger connotation, captures a situation in which there are practically no disincentives to extortion, theft, and murder, simply because anyone who cares to plan his crimes with a modicum of care faces no threat of being apprehended. Contract killings are virtually never punished. Between 1994 and mid-1997 none was successfully investigated and not a single arrest was made.[12]

Such blindness to problems of public order is scarcely unique to liberal Russian politicians. The intimacy of the link between order and genuine freedom forms a central tenet of virtually all versions of classical liberalism, as is amply evident in the writings of Locke, Kant, von Humboldt, and J. S. Mill. But many contemporary Western liberals, at the cost of their own doctrinal impoverishment and political decline, have renounced the supremacy of adamantine legal constraint and forsworn the responsibility inherent in Theodore Lowi's statement that "the intrinsic governmental feature is *legitimate use of coercion*." As Lowi argued some thirty years ago in his prescient, withering critique, contemporary American liberalism, in part by renouncing the necessity and centrality of coercion in the operation of government, virtually ensured a rise in public disorder, a decline in state autonomy and capacity, and an emasculation of public administration itself—even as the size of the administrative apparatus burgeoned.[13]

In the United States and other Western countries the growth of a one-sided liberalism has taken a gruesome toll on public order, interpersonal trust, and public confidence in government. Still, in most of the West, market economies and reasonably well-functioning regulatory institutions predated the transformation of liberalism from a doctrine of the rule of law into an ideology of perpetual accommodation and adjustment. What is more, the decline in severity of sanctions against gravely destructive behavior has not necessarily spelled the total elimination of deterrence. Murderers may no longer have much reason to expect that they will meet with the fate that Kant regarded as a moral imperative (execution), and well-to-do swindlers may expect exquisitely clement treatment and even retention of much of their ill-gotten fortunes. But the chance that they will be caught and suffer some punishment persists. The law may have become a soft constraint in liberal societies in the West, but it remains a constraint. In the realm of contract enforcement, moreover, the law continues to operate reasonably well and to guarantee orderly transaction in most Western societies.

In Russia, in contrast, the market itself was born into an environment in which the state assumed little responsibility for countervailing either crimes against persons or violations of contract. The most salient consequence, and one that serves as a hallmark of the racket economy, was the rapid, luxuriant growth of private protection rackets whose *post facto* eradication would now require much more coercive force, imagination, and political will than would have the *propter hoc* prevention of their emergence. The extent of coverage and depth of penetration of the post-Soviet Russian economy by such protection rackets knows no parallel in either Soviet times or periods of early capitalist development in the West. As Gregory Grossman demonstrates convincingly in his analysis of the Soviet underground in this volume, economic criminality and mutual dependence between state officials and private economic actors were hardly unknown during the Soviet period. Indeed, Grossman's pioneering work over the course of a quarter century of research revealed an underground economy in the Soviet Union that analysts in the West theretofore had scarcely known existed. But the extent of racketization during Soviet times was far less extensive than that prevailing in the post-Soviet period. Under the old regime the state was, at certain sites and during certain times, penetrated and corrupted by private interests. But the state nevertheless remained in the business of law enforcement and especially personal protection against violence—even if enforcement was uneven in practice and even if the laws themselves inhibited market formation. What is more, comparisons that liken the present Russian situation to periods of early capitalist development in the United States overestimate the extent of lawlessness in the latter case and underestimate it in the former case. Despite the justifiable celebrity of "robber baron capitalism" in the United States (and, in a variety of guises, in much of Europe as well), a complex system of criminal and civil law, courts, and law enforcement agencies nevertheless operated in the United States and in much of Europe even during capitalism's "wildest" phases. Unlike in present-day Russia, law enforcement did not—at least not on the scale of the territory of entire countries, including capital cities—become an entirely private matter.[14]

The withdrawal of the state from law enforcement and the consequent fantastic growth of protection rackets in Russia has a number of noteworthy economic consequences. It poisons the climate for investment by augmenting the cost of starting and operating a business—particularly in production and retail sales, where assets and employees normally must be "stationary" in a literal sense and therefore completely visible and vulnerable to predatory "protectors." Foreign firms must take into account the high state of physical danger in which their employees will find themselves, adding to the costs—and greatly reducing the attractiveness—of direct investment in Russia. The results are the two problems that Manuel Castells, in his contribution to this volume, rightly portrays as Russia's most devastating sources of economic paralysis: paltry rates of investment and prodigious capital flight. The breakdown of law enforcement also powerfully aggravates the problem of noncollection of taxes. State officials' unwillingness—or, now, in the cases of willing officials, inability—to coerce tax-evading enterprises ensures gross shortfalls in government revenues. At least among the managers and owners of large enterprises, no one ever suffers punishment for tax evasion in Russia. Evading taxes is scarcely more risky than committing extortion or murder.

The hidden hand of the market in post-Soviet Russia has its index finger on the trigger of a Kalashnikov. But it did not have to be that way. Allowing law enforcement to wither was a matter of policy, though those responsible cannot possibly have intended the results that ensued. The "requirements of primitive capital accumulation" or the "dictates of early capitalism" certainly are not to blame. Serious problems of crime and corruption are ubiquitous in societies undergoing rapid economic transformation. But where states do not wholly cast off their law enforcement responsibilities—be they in early nineteenth-century America, mid-nineteenth-century Germany and Japan, or for that matter post-Communist Poland, Mongolia, and Croatia—the criminalization of the entire economy and the collapse of public order in general did not accompany the advent of capitalism.

THE MORAL VACUUM

The fourth root of the racket economy is found in the absence, particularly in the political and economic elite but also to a lesser extent among the general population, of anything resembling a moral or ethical sense in matters connected with public life.[15] In broadest general terms, in any society two major mechanisms, aside from the fear of punishment, constrain individual human behavior: guilt, or the feeling of discomfort that arises from violating the internalized norms that are properly regarded as "conscience"; and shame, the aversive emotion that one encounters as a result of experiencing disgrace or the disapproval of others. Like most predominantly Christian cultures of the time, nineteenth- and early twentieth-century Russia had to some degree developed a guilt-culture, a way of life in which conscience, which may be understood as the core of morality itself, partially regulated human interaction. As Ferenc Fehér, Agnes Heller, and György Márkus explain in their still matchless dissection of the character of Soviet-type socialism, however, Bolshevik morality in Russia arrested the development of conscience while introducing a peculiar form of "shame culture" in which "morality" came to be based on two supreme virtues: loyalty and obedience to the Party. Disgrace in the eyes of the Party, at least for many Communists, represented not merely a threat to one's practical interests, but a genuine, sometimes agonizing source of personal shame. Thus, shame came to be "internalized" and to take on some of the traits normally associated with guilt, though shorn of the element of individual conscience as it is normally understood. While such a culture prevailed thoroughly only among true-believing Communists, it nevertheless permeated all levels of society, particularly in the birthplace of Bolshevism and its morality, Russia itself.[16] It provided a psychological basis for social control. Its effectiveness for this purpose, of course, began to wane well before the end of the Soviet era, but only during the Gorbachev era did the Party's self-proclaimed standing as "the reason, honor, and conscience of our era" evaporate completely, even in the minds and psyches of Party members and leaders themselves. The collapse of the Party would not necessarily have left Russian society so barren of anything resembling morality and conscience—except for the important detail, misunderstood or overlooked by observers who erroneously conceived of the Soviet regime in terms of "Marxist ideology" or as a vehicle of "modernization" and "development," that "Soviet morality" was based exclusively on all-embracing loyalty and obedience to the Party. It was not based on any values or norms that transcended the organization itself. What is more, the Party's status as the "reason, honor, and conscience of our era" could be achieved even imperfectly only through the estrangement of genuine, individual conscience. Thus, the dissolution of the Party-regime did not just bring down a political system; it swept away the only locus of unrepressed morality in society. Herein lies the deeper but often poorly understood foundation for the pedestrian, oft-heard observations that post-Soviet Russian society "doesn't believe in anything" or that it suffers from a "crisis of faith."

None of this is to argue that contemporary Russians are amoral in all aspects of life; they certainly are not. It is just to say that Russian society lacks anything resembling normative-moral codes in matters relevant to economics and politics. Civic morals and norms that are taken for granted in public life and economic interaction in many other societies, in Europe and North America as well as in parts of Asia and Latin America, are virtually impossible to find in Russia. The implication of this state of affairs is devastating. As Durkheim rightly asserted in his searching analysis of the connection between individual and group interests, "There is no form of social activity which can do without the appropriate moral discipline."[17] Social activity in the realm of the economy is no exception.

In the vast majority of modern societies the principal sources of norms and ethics relevant to public life are religious tradition and communal solidarity. With regard to religious tradition, what matters most is not whether all or most citizens are presently devoted to religious doctrines, but rather whether a commitment to a transcendental good and a set of principles that are not subject to sudden change based on instrumental calculation or the whims of rulers has suffused the life of society and exerted lingering effects, whatever the extent of modern secularization. In few if any societies do lofty ethics directly steer the conduct of politicians and economic actors. Yet, to a greater extent than is often recognized, legal norms, public expectations of leaders and leaders' feel for public opinion, the way that citizens conceive of leadership, followership, and responsibility, and interaction in the realm of the economy are deeply influenced by at least the residue of ethical systems derived from religious tradition. Virtually every aspect of public life in the United States, even at the end of the twentieth century, is shaped by Christian and Jewish traditions; the same may be said for Islam in Malaysia and Buddhism in Thailand. But in Russia, Orthodox and all other religious-ethical traditions were ground to dust by the Communist regime. Mere marginalization or neglect would not do; full decimation, including the physical liquidation of much of the priesthood and its replacement in many cases with actual agents of the state security agencies dressed in clerical garb, was demanded by the logic of the Party's own morality. "Reason, honor, and conscience," after all, are not divisible quantities that may be compromised or shared. No potential competitors that might have some claim on them could be allowed to function.

The shallowness and even artificiality of the revival of Orthodoxy in post-Soviet Russia testify to the extent and duration of decimation. The absence of a genuine interest in Orthodoxy or other faiths among the vast majority of young and middle-aged Russians, despite a fleeting semblance of revival at the time of communism's demise, bespeaks not merely a need for "modernization" of the church's appeal and the presence of too many eccentric long-beards in the clergy. It demonstrates that the very tradition of religious (or at least Orthodox) thought has been extinguished for decades.[18] The farcical efforts of political leaders, including those of the (atheist) president, the (atheist) leader of the largest opposition party, the (atheist) governor of Krasnoyarsk who is often regarded as the country's most popular politician, and the (atheist) mayor of Moscow (the last of whom has spent one-half billion dollars to rebuild a gargantuan, gold-encrusted cathedral as a monument to his own power) to resuscitating the church as a national *symbol* demonstrate time and again just how defunct Orthodoxy is as a socially and intellectually relevant tradition. Despite a powerful and systematic seventy-year effort, the old regime certainly did not succeed in instilling real atheism in the population, as is evident in the survival and flourishing of every conceivable form of spiritualism and superstition in post-Soviet Russia. But the regime did manage to obliterate Orthodoxy, both morally and organizationally, thus bequeathing to post-Soviet Russia a society in which God may not be dead (and the gods and the astrologers certainly are not) but where the formerly supreme source of moral learning, education, and inspiration has been defunct for generations. Other religious traditions scarcely fared better. The revival of Judaism that is reported to be occurring among hundreds of Muscovites takes place in the wake of an exodus of hundreds of thousands for a homeland in the Middle East, where the already settled population is continually struck by the new arrivals' ignorance of and disinterest in anything that smacks of religious teaching, learning, or practice.[19]

It is impossible directly to demonstrate the effects of the decimation of religious tradition on the economy in Russia. But it is noteworthy that in post-Communist societies where ethical traditions rooted in religious principles and organizations were not so thoroughly demolished, such as in Poland, the Baltic states of the former Soviet Union, Hungary, and Slovenia, the criminalization of public life and of the economy in particular, despite the usual traumas of transition, has not even approached levels found in Russia.

In the realm of communal solidarity Russia faces a similar state of desolation. The aspect of communal solidarity that matters most for modern society's ability to minimize the growth of social pathologies while enduring social stress and dislocation is the depth and nature of commitment to the welfare of the broader national community, which may serve as a rough definition of patriotism. Patriotism is, despite superficial appearances, in extremely short supply in post-Soviet Russia. There is no dearth of "patriotic" noise. But the timbre of the hue and cry reveals the weakness of genuine patriotism. Mighty governmental exertions and state-sponsored contests to define the "Russian idea," harsh nationalist rhetoric from leaders of virtually every political stripe, and a prestige-obsessed foreign policy intent on little other than gaining external recognition of enduring national greatness may seem to evince the potency of patriotism. But this is the nationalism of Vichy, not De Gaulle.[20] Exclusionary, scapegoat-seeking, self-pitying, defensive, xenophobic, and nostalgic, it neither embodies nor inspires a spirit of sacrifice or self-reliance for the sake of the broader community. The Latvian population enduring a frigid winter with scant natural gas rather than yielding a shred of recently won national sovereignty; Koreans giving up precious personal possessions to enable their country better to withstand national economic emergency; most Chinese students returning home after receiving their advanced degrees in the United States without attempting immigration to the West—these acts embody a type of patriotism that helps carry societies through hard times. Comparable large-scale acts of individual sacrifice for the national good are inconceivable in present-day Russia.

Accounting for the weakness of genuine patriotism in Russia is not easy. Russia's place as the central entity and maker of a recently collapsed empire and the intimacy with which Russian national identity has long been tied to its imperial identity (which contrasts with, say, British national identity, which always existed comfortably in separation from Britain's overseas holdings) may provide a partial explanation. So too may the legacy of the peculiar way that Soviet rulers exploited Russian nationalism while undermining the development of a distinct and robust Russian national identity.

Whatever its causes, the vapidity of nationalism and the absence of a constructive sense of national purpose compromise Russians' ability collectively to endure the strains of transformation and have direct and dire implications for the economy. Not only can leaders count on none of the kind of invaluable popular sacrifice evident in the behavior of the Latvians, Koreans, and Chinese mentioned above, but also leaders themselves pay so little heed to national interests in their decisions on economic policy that entire national industries that could be supported or saved with little effort are sacrificed without a second thought. Nothing could better demonstrate the consequences of the dearth of enlightened patriotism than Manuel Castells's poignant account in his contribution to this volume of the destruction of the personal computer industry in Zelenograd in the mid-1990s. In this case, legislators—including, incidentally, many who claim strong "patriotic" credentials by virtue of their xenophobia—accepted the blandishments extended by the trading companies' lobby and voted for a law that destroyed the competitive advantage of a manufacturer located in Russia. The act effectively ceded the Russian market for personal computers to East Asian manufacturers. Given Zelenograd's earlier potential as the nucleus of a Russian Silicon Valley and the devastating impact of parliament's decision on employment and earnings in the city, the lawmakers' behavior betrays how unpatriotic Russian nationalism can be and how devastating this can be for the economy.

THE DEBILITY OF SOCIETAL ORGANIZATION

The racket economy is also rooted in the frailty of societal organizations. Russia suffers not only from an acute deficit of the *traditions and commitments,* both religious and national, that may constrain the criminalization of society and the economy. It also labors under a shortage of the *organizational forms* that typically also perform such tasks. Russia is living through Durkheim's nightmare—a predicament in which society generates new forms of associability far more slowly than economic change dissolves older forms of solidarity and induces social dislocation.[21]

This conundrum is novel or at least unusual in Russia. Before 1917, the nobility, the clergy, the often angry and dissident intelligentsia, and the communal setting in which peasants made their lives provided frameworks that established bonds of social cohesion and regulated behavior. In the Soviet era these social groups were washed away, but they were replaced by organizational and communal forms that recreated, albeit on entirely different foundations, group membership and social cohesion. The crucial organizational form that established status relations that cemented rulers together and bounded the ruled to them was of course the Communist Party and its auxiliary organizations. The army was another organization that generated social cement. The Soviet intelligentsia, as artificial as it might have seemed to many in the West, also served as an important locus of social cohesion. The Soviet state's consistent policy of total statization, however, blocked the emergence of autonomous organizations of civil society such as political parties, charitable organizations, trade unions, and professional associations.

In post-Soviet circumstances, the sources of social cohesion that the Soviet regime created disintegrated completely, while the legacy of repression of nonstate organization left Russia with a society extremely poor in the intermediaries that typically structure social, political, and economic life in many other countries. The Communist Party is now just a political party like any other. Its membership stands at only about one-thirtieth of what it did at the end of the Soviet period. By the mid-1990s genuine programmatic parties had come into being and begun to structure political competition on the national level. But membership in parties encompasses less than one percent of the total population, and no party has generated subsidiary organizations that can serve as real sources of social cohesion. The army has been laid to waste as an organization and as a source of status and positive group identification. The Soviet-era intelligentsia, such as it was, dissolved as it lost its formerly privileged position in society—even as many of its members as individuals prospered handsomely under post-Soviet conditions. Political parties, trade unions, professional associations, "good government" associations, and other such intermediaries have indeed begun to emerge in post-Soviet Russia. But they started virtually from scratch and have not acquired the power and stature needed to serve as potent, weighty factors in political and economic life.[22]

For the purposes of the present article, the most important consequences of civil-societal weakness are extreme difficulties in holding the powerful accountable and in generating bona fide political choice. The weakness of independent trade unions and professional associations means that grasping enterprise administrators and local officials rarely encounter formidable organized resistance to their schemes for embezzling revenues, loans, and grants and then claiming that they do not have enough cash on hand to meet payroll. The underdevelopment of political parties deprives the political system of precisely those organizations that often are most concerned with and capable of reducing corrupt practices among politicians. The British system lacks an American-style division of powers and mutual oversight between executives and legislators. But the leaders of parties, concerned with their organizations' reputations among voters, often monitor their own members, including parliamentarians, even if such efforts are not always successful. Political parties in Chile similarly have a long tradition of monitoring and disciplining their own members for the sake of maintaining a reputation for probity.[23] Russia's parties are not sufficiently strong and well integrated to carry out such functions.

Ineffectual parties also severely restrict the ability of the political process to offer voters real choice. The 1996 presidential election offers a case in point. Particularly given the executive-heavy nature of the regime, the election was of supreme importance for the country's future. The absence of a liberal party with a strong national organization greatly reduced the viability of a liberal alternative. Grigorii Iavlinskii, whose Iabloko party did not even have enough activists to mount a serious grassroots campaign in most regions, finished with a mere 7 percent in the first round. Despite his personal fame and consistent reputation as Russia's "most popular politician," Aleksandr Lebed, due to the absence of the backing of a strong political party, managed only one-seventh of the vote and failed to make the second round. No strong Christian democratic or social democratic parties of any appreciable size or strength were found on the Russian political field. The presidential race therefore by default came down to a clear—but to most voters, unappealing—choice between a deeply flawed and unpopular incumbent and the even less appealing leader of the country's only large and well structured party, the Communist Party of the Russian Federation.[24] American citizens often express dissatisfaction with the choices they face on election day. But it would be difficult to find an American presidential race that pitted one candidate who favored destroying democratic institutions against one who was so debilitated that he spent more than half of his time in office away from work and in seclusion, coping with illnesses and personal problems about which the public was regularly misinformed. The American system of primaries, run by the major parties, does not always put forward candidates about which the majority of the electorate feels genuine enthusiasm. But it does produce nominees who combine considerable personal vigor with demonstrated political prowess.

In sum, five major factors converged to produce a racket economy in Russia. The country's extraordinarily rich endowment in natural resources encouraged the concentration of wealth, rent-seeking in low-value-added sectors rather than the promotion of industry, and the formation of especially cozy relationships between private interests and officialdom. The character of economic reform, and privatization in particular, further concentrated wealth and institutionalized relationships of intimate interdependence between public officials and private capitalists by establishing an oligarchy of financial-industrial groups. The government's shedding of law-enforcement functions ensured that protection would become a private affair. It thereby guaranteed that competition among the new oligarchs would often be violent, that the new economy would be blanketed with protection rackets, and that the citizenry in general would be left virtually unprotected by the law. The moral vacuum, stemming largely from the decimation of religious traditions and communal solidarities, in combination with the frailty and novelty of autonomous civil-societal organizations, left society and the polity bereft of bastions of moral or organizational resistance to criminalization.

RUSSIA IN COMPARATIVE PERSPECTIVE

The confluence of these factors is highly unusual. Among post-Communist countries, which serve as the most proximate comparative referents, it is difficult to find other cases in which all five conditions are clearly present. Table 1 provides a rough picture of the presence or absence of the factors discussed above in the post-Communist region. It involves numerous judgment calls. For example, one can scarcely determine precisely whether or not a society suffers from a politically and economically relevant moral deficit. The table is included only as an imperfect aid to placing Russia in a broader comparative perspective.

Among post-Communist countries, only Azerbaijan, Kazakhstan, and Turkmenistan enjoy—or are cursed by—endowments of natural resources that compare to those found in Russia. Assessing whether the logic of privatization programs created oligarchies and concentrations of wealth analogous to those found in Russia is extremely difficult and adequate data are still scarce. Several facts,

Table 1

Roots of the Racket Economy

Country	Extraordinary Natural Resource Endowment	Privatization that Creates New Oligarchy	Withdrawal of the State from Law Enforcement	Moral Vacuum	Weak Societal Organization
Albania		x	x	x	x
Armenia		x			x
Azerbaijan	x			x	x
Belarus				x	x
Bosnia			x	x	x
Bulgaria				x	x
Croatia		x			
Czech Republic					x
Estonia					x
Georgia			x		x
Hungary					
Kazakhstan	x	x		x	x
Kyrgyz Republic		x		x	x
Latvia					x
Lithuania					x
Macedonia		x			
Moldova		x			x
Mongolia					x
Poland					
Romania		x		x	x
Russia	x	x	x	x	x
Serbia				x	
Slovakia					x
Slovenia					
Tajikistan		x	x	x	x
Turkmenistan	x			x	x
Ukraine				x	x
Uzbekistan				x	x

however, stand out clearly. First, economic change in the "most reformed" economies—those in which privatization and liberalization proceeded the most rapidly and extensively—did not produce the pathologies found in Russia. Purely economic inequalities have increased since the demise of socialism in all countries in the region. Yet in the countries that reformed most resolutely and quickly, including Poland, Czechoslovakia, the Baltic states, Hungary, and Slovenia, the advent of capitalism manifestly has not brought the extent of oligarchization or the explosion of income and wealth differentials evident in Russia.[25] Privatization programs in these countries differed widely, but all of them included mechanisms designed to spread wealth over a substantial portion of the population. None of them were based on loans-for-shares schemes that involved virtual giveaways of enormous chunks of assets, nor on other mechanisms that guaranteed full oligarchization via the creation of enormous financial-industrial conglomerates. Interestingly, albeit perhaps unsurprisingly, none of the "least reformed" economies produced the type of oligarchies found in Russia either. Azerbaijan, Belarus, Tajikistan, Turkmenistan, and Uzbekistan simply did not carry out enough privatization to allow for the formation of Russian-type FIGs. Rulers thwarted economic de-Sovietization and maintained strict state control. Doing so engendered its own set of economic and social disasters but also prevented the type of oligarichization found in Russia.

Russian-style withdrawal of the state from law enforcement occurred only in a handful of other cases. In most of these, such as Georgia until 1996 and Tajikistan throughout the post-Soviet period, civil wars destroyed states' capacities to engage in basic law enforcement. In some other cases, such as Bulgaria, Kazakhstan, and Moldova, declining state capacities led to serious deterioration in public order, but the state did not abandon public protection entirely. The only other case that closely resembled Russia, insofar as a government eschewed law enforcement not merely as a result of incapacity but due also to highly idealistic liberal assumptions on the part of policymakers, was Albania under the ultraliberal-turned-authoritarian president, Sali Berisha. In most other cases, either democratic governments managed to combine commitments to political and economic freedom with efforts aimed at avoiding the dissolution of public order, or authoritarian or semidemocratic governments eschewed liberalism while assigning great importance to maintaining order. Poland, Latvia, and Estonia serve as examples of the former; Belarus after 1994, Uzbekistan, and Croatia as examples of the latter.

Assessing precisely whether or not a given society has or lacks moral foundations for political and economic behavior is of course impossible. But it is probably not controversial to say that most of the countries of Eastern Europe, the Baltics, and the Caucasus remained deeply influenced even through the Soviet period by either hardy religious traditions or strong traditions of individual commitment to the nation or both. Poland, Estonia, Armenia, Croatia, Slovenia, and Hungary provide clear examples of societies where both survived Sovietism intact. The Slavic and Central Asian republics of the former Soviet Union are probably the places where traditions of religious commitment and national solidarity were the most thoroughly decimated (or most effectively prevented from emerging) by the Communist regime. These societies now find themselves trapped in a moral and ethical vacuum that conduces criminalization.

Finally, it is reasonably safe to say that most of the countries in the region entered the post-Communist period with very weak infrastructures of autonomous organizations. Poland presented the only unambiguous case of a vigorous civil society. Hungary and countries of the former Yugoslavia probably merit inclusion in the category of countries where civil society was not entirely leveled. The Czech Republic and the Baltic states of the former Soviet Union are marginal cases that defy easy classification. The other countries, however, cannot be said to have begun their post-Communist lives with anything other than weak or nonexistent civil societies.

In short, the factors that gave rise to the racket economy in Russia are not individually or in various combinations unusual, but the presence of all five in a single country is. A special word is in order about Ukraine, a country that is often regarded as similar to Russia. Ukraine lacks the natural resource endowment found in Russia. Interestingly, however, the one part of Ukraine that is rich in resources—the eastern region in and around Donetsk and Dnepropetrovsk, which is endowed with precious metals—has by far the most serious problem with economic criminalization. Like in many parts of Russia, near total corruption of officialdom and gangland-style assassinations among competing mafias are common in the region.[26] Still, Ukraine clearly lacks a Russian-scale endowment of natural resources. On the other hand, the moral vacuum and the societal-organizational weaknesses found in Russia characterize Ukraine as well. In the realm of economic change, Ukraine's first post-Soviet government, that of President Leonid Kravchuk, undertook so little economic reform that it, like most of the Bulgarian governments leading up to the triumph of the reformist coalition in Bulgaria in 1997, did not really establish the basis for the type of oligarchy that emerged in Russia. Like in Bulgaria, however, the Ukrainian government's lack of commitment to privatization did not block entirely the formation of an economic oligarchy. It just restricted the scope of its development and ensured that the "new" oligarchy would resemble that of the Soviet era. The change of power in Ukraine that followed the victory of Leonid Kuchma in the presidential elections of 1994 did lead to some efforts at economic destatization. The initial phase of Kuchma's plan in many ways resembled the first stage of Russia's privatization, including a general distribution of vouchers. It is not yet clear whether Ukraine's program will follow the path of Russia's and produce similar structural results in the economy.[27] Unlike in Russia but like in Bulgaria, private banks remain small and weak in Ukraine; nothing resembling the flush and mighty financial behemoths that dominate Russia's economy has yet emerged.

Placing Russia in a broader cross-national framework reveals that the country is unusual, even within the post-Communist region. Such a discussion raises an exceedingly complex question: *Why* is Russia distinctive? Does Russia's lone possession of all five of the causes of racketization represent an inauspicious but largely accidental conjunction of circumstances, or can the country's distinctiveness be understood in terms of some underlying, unifying factor? Attempting to identify and explicate such a factor entails hazards and requires considerable extension and elaboration of the current discussion, but it may help furnish deeper and more thoroughly comparative insight into the Russian condition.

It is noteworthy that the roots of the racket all may be traced, directly or indirectly, to the legacy of Soviet rule, and particularly to the type of Sovietism that prevailed in Russia by virtue of that country's status as the primogenitor, the keeper, and the center of Sovietism itself. Upon first examination, it appears that several of the roots of racketization are consequences of Soviet legacies and others are the results of post-Soviet political choices. In fact, however, even the latter ultimately may be traced to the former—even if some of the specific policy choices made by Russia's post-Soviet rulers cannot and should not be blamed exclusively on the Soviet past. That past did not fully determine policies in the post-Soviet situation. In a probabilistic sense, however, even some crucial decisions made after August 1991 can be understood largely in terms of prior conditions. The first root of the racket, Russia's superabundance of raw materials, is structural. But the country's hyperdependence on the proceeds from raw materials production is the consummation of decades of Soviet-era policy. The fourth and fifth roots of the racket economy, the moral vacuum and the weakness of societal organization, are, unsurprisingly, unusually acute in Russia due to the duration and intensity of sovietization in Russia and the predominance of Russians in the construction and direction of the Soviet system itself.[28] The peculiar shame culture discussed above undoubtedly reached a higher state of entrenchment and elaboration in the homeland of Bolshevism than in most other Soviet republics, and a still higher state than anywhere in Eastern Europe, which endured less than a decade of Stalinism and only about forty years of sovietization. Furthermore, Russia was the only country in the region—though Ukraine was clear second—where national consciousness and organizations, in official thinking, propaganda, and planning, were entirely submerged in Soviet consciousness and organizations and where virtually any manifestations of nationalism, or for that matter religious or other nonpolitical cultural expression, were regarded as grave threats to Sovietism itself.[29] The decimation of independent organizational life was also carried out more thoroughly and consistently in Russia than in most other countries. Even countries in the Soviet Union itself, including the three major countries of the Caucasus and the three of the Baltic region, did not experience the extent of decimation of nonstate organization that Russia did. In Eastern Europe, only the regimes of Nicolae Ceauşescu Romania and of Enver Hoxha in Albania managed to squash society as thoroughly as Russia's rulers did, but in both of these countries Sovietism's lifespan was far shorter than in Russia.

The Soviet-Russian origins of the second and third roots of the racket, the character of economic reform and the withdrawal of the state from law enforcement, are not as intuitively obvious. A full understanding of these factors nevertheless also requires consideration of Russia's singular heritage. The immediate post-Soviet government's decisions on the economy reflected a peculiarly post-Soviet Russian form of liberalism that was at once passionately libertarian, highly optimistic, and supremely self-assured. The zealotry of the early reformers originated in sharp, diametric opposition to Sovietism itself, which found its purest incarnation in Russia. Russia created the highest manifestations of Sovietism and so also the most fertile ground for the genesis of their purest opposites.[30] Just as liberal leaders such as Gaidar initially even shunned political parties because they regarded the very idea of party organization and discipline as "Soviet," so in the economic realm they pursued radically un-Soviet policies, which in practice meant the most rapid possible privatization of property. Gaidar and his associates correctly grasped that the essence of Sovietism in the economy was the abolition of private property. So their desire to destatize as quickly as possible was consistent with an acute understanding of the nature of Sovietism and its antithesis. But privatizing the lion's share of the world's fifth (or seventh or eighth, depending on how one calculates) economy within a few short years required some extraordinary methods. Thus, when voucher privatization managed to create only the rudiments of a privatized economy, another method had to be turned to immediately in order to accelerate destatization. The zealotry of the reformers meant that speed and "irreversibility" were of the essence, and the fastest way to dump state assets was precisely that—to dump them, to sell them so cheaply that finding buyers, even under the extraordinarily risky conditions that prevailed at the time, would not be the least bit problematic.

Finding buyers fast—rather than finding the "right" or "strategic" buyers, those whose purchases would maximize revenues to the state, those who would be the most likely to initiate restructuring, or even those who would most richly reward government officials—was what loans-for-shares was all about. There is no question that high-ranking government officials personally benefited from the scheme and that many of the investors who profited the most handsomely had strong connections to officialdom. There is also no question that the consequences of the program included economic oligarchization. But since the whole idea of selling off government property as quickly as possible originated early in the privatization program and was driven largely by a zealous anti-Soviet economic ideology, an analysis that focuses exclusively on interests and ignores the ideational underpinnings of how the program even came to be possible neglects a potentially crucial dimension of the story. Anatolii Chubais might have benefited personally from the scheme in material terms. Indeed, there is evidence that he turned deceitful and corrupt as the 1990s wore on. But his initial zeal and the force with which he rammed the loans-for-shares program through were not driven only, or even primarily, by a desire to maximize revenues accruing to himself. What is more, there is little evidence that the ultimate guardian of the program, Yeltsin himself, was motivated by a desire for personal material gain. Even most of Yeltsin's harshest critics train their fire on his alleged incompetence; few would accuse him of having designed policies with an eye toward filling a Swiss bank account of his own. Yeltsin may have become too feeble to carry out his responsibilities effectively, but he has never been a Marcos or a Suharto.

If the libertarian devotion of the liberals' economic program may be traced to their fervent desire to create the very opposite of the version of Sovietism that they knew best, which was its purest, oldest, *Russian* version, their wild optimism regarding the anticipated results of destatization and their underestimation of the dangers of oligarchization may be attributed in part to their near complete lack of understanding of how market economies actually work. Again, observers who see only cynicism and naked self-interest in the liberals' every move overlook an important driving force in the entire economic reform project. Gaidar, Yeltsin, Chubais, former finance minister Boris Federov, and other architects of the great economic transformation simply had no idea what the effects of their reforms would be. Unlike their counterparts in, say, Poland, Hungary, Slovenia, Croatia, and perhaps even the Caucasus, they had no personal feel for what a market of any type looked like, except for what they gleaned from the handful of Western economics textbooks and relevant philosophical tracts that were available in Moscow in the 1980s—much as few Western observers really ever understood what a socialist economy or enterprise looked like. None of the new liberal leaders who assumed control of the executive branch in 1991–92 had earned degrees in the West or even spent a significant amount of time there. Gaidar enjoyed some foreign experience, but his expertise was in Yugoslavia; his best foreign language was Serbo-Croatian. Such a state of affairs was hardly surprising. The Russia in which these young reformers grew up and were educated was one of the world's most isolated and closed societies. Until the Gorbachev era, it was a place where historians and philosophers specializing on Lev Trotsky were required to write harsh critiques of Trotsky's shameful revisions and deviations, but were forced to rely exclusively on other secondary critiques since they were never allowed to see Trotsky's own writings, access to which was granted only to high-ranking members of the academic nomenklatura. The Russian reformers' ignorance made them naive about how to move from plan to market without setting the stage for disasters.

And still, these were anything but dull, uneducated, or unimaginative people. Despite their naiveté, born of inexperience and lack of exposure, they constituted a highly intelligent and energetic cadre (or separate circles of cadres) who knew what they wanted and at least thought that they knew how to get it. In this respect, Moscow's status as imperial center and thus home of many of the region's most talented and confident leaders is of great importance.[31] Gaidar, Chubais, and Federov—and for that matter, Gennadii Burbulis, Aleksandr Shokhin, Petr Aven, Ella Pamfilova, and Grigorii Iavlinskii—were naturally in the center, in Moscow, at the time of transition. Analogous figures were not to be found—at least not in a quantity that could have created a self-confident, pioneering liberal political class—in, say, Kiev, Tbilisi, Alma-Ata, Minsk, Baku, Skopje, or Bucharest at the beginning of transitions. In sum, Russia's early post-Communist economic policymakers combined zealotry spurred by reaction to what they intended to destroy, naiveté born of ignorance of what they intended to build, and confidence and talent stemming from their status as inhabitants of what had been the region's intellectual and political capital. Only Russia, by virtue of what it had been during the Soviet period, thrust to power a cadre of post-Soviet leaders who carried such a peculiar and paradoxical set of traits. And only such leaders could have carried out the highly distinctive brand of reform seen in Russia during the early post-Communist period.

The same combination of reactive ideological ardor, ignorance-induced guilelessness, and energetic, youthful confidence shaped early post-Soviet Russian leaders' approaches to law enforcement. In a nutshell, and with only a modicum of exaggeration, one may state that Russia's immediate post-Soviet leaders simply did not see the need for concern with law enforcement. The law in Soviet Russia served as the codification of the state's subordination of the individual; it was anything but a tool for safeguarding individuals' rights.[32] Russia's crusading post-Soviet liberal leaders, given their prior experience with "the law" and their counter-Soviet, libertarian faith that individuals have far more to fear from the state than from other private individuals and organizations, were led to regard law enforcement itself with suspicion.[33] It caused them to neglect the tasks of rebuilding, depoliticizing, modernizing, and reshaping the agencies of coercion in favor of defunding, emasculating, and for the most part simply ignoring them. What is more, the unschooled faith of the new libertarians in the market, and their reflexive and oft-expressed association of the market with "civilized countries," led them to view the market itself as an antidote to crime and disorder, or at worst as an institution that would eventually organize disorder in a manner that would greatly mitigate its harmful effects. So far from grasping that the release of new entrepreneurial forces under conditions of general societal breakdown would actually require refurbished, better equipped, more authoritative, and in general stronger and better organized agencies of public order, post-Soviet leaders' actions and inaction demonstrated that they simply did not see revitalizing law enforcement agencies as a necessary component of market-building.[34] It is not impossible to see how the new leaders' combination of faith in the market, ignorance of the intimacy of the tie between "the market" and "civilization," on the one hand, and coercive state power on the other, and their boundless confidence in their own ability to read the situation accurately and to respond effectively to any contingency produced a policy toward the agencies of coercion that very likely felt to the leaders themselves like enlightened benign neglect, but that in practice turned out to have truly malign consequences. And again, as in the case of economic reform, it is possible to perceive how the custodians of the new Russian state, precisely by virtue of their backgrounds and status as Russians, differed in their ideologies, perspectives, attitudes, and self-images from their counterparts in the other countries of the post-Communist region.

THE WAY OUT OF THE RACKET

Given the multifaceted foundations and the deep entrenchment of the racket economy, racketization may appear to be irreversible in Russia. The country may be condemned to endure indefinitely the least felicitous features of stifling statism and bare-knuckle capitalism. Indeed, rapid transformation of the Russian economy into a "normal" market in the near future may be ruled out. It must be borne in mind that the Russian economy faces a bundle of technical problems that would pose daunting challenges even under the best of circumstances. The necessity to reduce dependence on primary products stands as a particularly pressing task, and one that many other countries at roughly similar levels of development have failed to resolve. Enterprise restructuring also remains a burning and thoroughly unresolved issue. In some cases privatization has created real owners with an interest in firms' productivity, but in general it has not exerted the propitious effects on restructuring that most government officials, analysts, and Western economists earlier anticipated. Enterprise restructuring has proven to be an enormously vexing obstacle to economic progress in most of the post-Communist world, including and in some respects especially in Russia. From Saxony to Ulan Bator, the level of dysfunction—or at least unreadiness to operate in a post-command environment—that was built into Soviet-type enterprises continues, nearly a decade after the onset of transitions, to bewilder those engaged in studying or attempting to reform them. As one leading scholar, in answer to a question on why multilateral lending institutions and foreign investors have encountered such enormous difficulties in their dealings with enterprises in post-Soviet Russia, aptly remarked, "I don't think that they knew or even know yet what a socialist enterprise really looked like."[35]

Diversification of production and enterprise restructuring serve as only two of the major problems plaguing the Russian economy. Building a reasonably well-functioning financial system also looms as another enormous challenge. The mere existence of large, powerful organizations that call themselves banks does not a modern financial system make. Perhaps the rapid emergence of such concerns gives Russia a head start over countries such as Bulgaria and Ukraine, where such institutions are simply absent. One might argue that at least the organizational infrastructure for a modern financial system exists in Russia. But in their current form, Russia's "financial institutions" do not really engage in "finance"—at least not in the way that this term is normally understood in the West, and certainly not in a manner that stimulates investment, production, and development. Few of Russia's banks actually engage in large-scale, long-term credit provision. Rather, they function as consumers of inexpensive state-emitted credits, money laundromats, currency speculation machines, purchasers and overlords of enterprises and communications facilities, and nerve-centers for the public-relations and political-career-promotion efforts of their owners and of allied politicians. Russian banks are many things—but they are not banks. Their existence scarcely resolves the problem of creating a modern financial system.

Such economic issues are the subjects of large and sophisticated literatures and cannot be investigated in any depth in the present paper.[36] These problems, as crucial as they are to the future of the Russian economy, however, are ultimately unresolvable in the absence of progress on the core problem: the creation of something resembling the rule of law in the market. Thus, as important as technical issues are and as much attention as they deservedly receive in the economics and political science literatures, in practice they are second-order problems. Movement away from dependence on primary products, enterprise restructuring on a scale that will alter the trajectory of economic development, and the growth of a modern financial system will not occur in the absence of some progress toward a rule of law in the market. Thus, measures designed to begin moving the economy from a state of full criminalization to one of partial criminalization are the crucial prerequisites for progress on technical problems such as those mentioned above. Such potential remedies are the topic of this section of the paper. The following subsection considers what types of changes are necessary, desirable, and feasible. The second subsection investigates the crucial question of agency—of *how* the necessary changes might be effected and *by whom.* The remedies proposed here derive logically, albeit not inexorably, from the causal diagnosis sketched above.

REDUCING THE RACKET: WHAT IS—AND IS NOT—TO BE DONE

Structural dependence on raw materials and extractive industries may be the least eradicable root of the racket economy. The best that can be hoped for in the foreseeable future is some diversification that would reduce the supremacy of fuels, metals, and minerals. Such a shift would require a fresh commitment by state officials to bolster potentially competitive, high-value-added manufactures such as aircraft, automobiles, military hardware, and computers. It would also necessitate a radical improvement in the climate for investment outside the energy and raw materials sectors.

Regarding the trajectory of economic reform, it is important to recognize that deprivatization of property, including that which was sold at criminally low prices during the loans-for-shares phase, is now impossible, at least without bloodshed. The FIGs and the companies that form their nuclei have hidden—in some cases not so hidden—private armies organized to resist any moves against their employers. Relatedly, in the realm of law enforcement, near-term radical change that could fully reverse the damage of the state's earlier neglect is probably not feasible, at least without the use of drastically illiberal and antidemocratic methods. Belated measures taken ostensibly to compensate for earlier neglect of law enforcement responsibilities, such as recent steps that effectively undermine habeas corpus and relegate petty criminals (or those accused of crimes) who cannot come up with bribe money to protracted pretrial detentions do not and will not put so much as a nick in the problem of racketization. Such misplaced, flimsy, and inappropriate measures simply throw into even bolder relief the bankruptcy of the current approach to law enforcement.[37]

The conundra that have arisen as consequences of privatization and the state's abandonment of its responsibility for maintaining order create the duel temptations of restatization in the economic realm and reversion to authoritarianism in the political sphere. But there are reasons beyond practical difficulties to regard each as unwise and counterproductive. Restatization—even supposing that the FIGs could be broken down and their assets seized, as many politicians both red and brown would like to do—would fail to crack criminalization while actually destroying what modest gains Russia has made in economic restructuring and performance. As discussed above, the least criminalized economies in the post-Communist world are the most reformed ones. Those that are now the most reformed, moreover, by no means "started" as the least criminalized. As one may infer from a close reading of Jadwiga Staniszkis's fascinating depiction of the socialist economy's disintegration during the final years of the Communist regime in Poland, without radical liberalization and rapid privatization (at least in trade and small and medium-sized enterprises) during the immediate post-Communist period, Poland very well may have developed one of the region's most criminalized economies.[38] By mid-1997, a leading Polish scholar and former high-ranking government official could remark, with full justification, "We Poles have a serious problem with economic crime and corruption. 'Serious', of course, is a relative term; compared to the Russians, we are innocent babes."[39] Much the same may be said of the Baltic states of the former Soviet Union. Thoroughgoing economic reform, rather than state control, has facilitated the emergence of the rule of law in the post-Communist world.

Maintenance of state ownership or efforts to reestablish it also represent dead ends in terms of economic performance. As I have shown in a cross-national analysis of the post-Communist region in a separate article, more privatization and greater liberalization have yielded better economic performance in terms of both inflation and growth rates. "Gradualism," be it of the Ukrainian, Bulgarian, Kazakh, Azeri, or other type, has spelled economic disaster, even by comparison with Russia's (at best) checkered record.[40] State ownership has only proliferated rent-seeking opportunities for politicians, burdened state coffers, and eliminated even the possibility of enterprise restructuring. The Chinese and Vietnamese experiences, moreover, which are often adduced by opponents of radical economic reform, are widely misinterpreted and misapplied. In fact, neither serves as a particularly good example of gradualism. Both countries actually undertook reforms that in some realms were more radical and thoroughgoing than those seen even in the most reformed economies of Eastern Europe. As James Riedel and Bruce Comer note, within just two years (1988–89), Vietnam effectively privatized the dominant sectors of its economy and achieved stabilization via a program that "was pure IMF orthodoxy, albeit without the IMF behind it."[41] Whether the state or some private entity owns and/or controls production, distribution, and service provision does matter, and the case for the state in transition economies is exceedingly weak. Indeed, the most formidable dissenters from the notion that ownership is not of great importance, or that state ownership may be superior, include not only Vietnamese leaders, but also the current Chinese government. The latter currently is demonstrating great willingness to incur substantial political risks, including further erosion of party control and expansion of autonomous economic power in society, in order to reap the enormous efficiency gains involved in accelerating the destatization of production, a process that is already well advanced.[42] Finally, the much less thorough interfirm and interregional interdependence and the much less onerous burden of the socialist welfare state's obligations in Vietnam and China relative to the post-Communist cases rule out an easy interpretation of the "lessons" of the Asian experiences, however one characterizes the Asian reforms.[43]

None of this is to argue that state enterprises can never be efficient and productive. As Stephen Cohen and Andrew Schwartz point out in their contribution to this volume, Western Europe is replete with successful state enterprises. But Cohen and Schwartz also rightly hold that state ownership is not to be sought as an end in itself. In the transition economies of the post-Communist world, as well as the "still Communist" countries of East Asia, this caveat, if anything, amounts to an understatement. In fact, further privatization (but privatization that is not controlled by its beneficiaries), and especially sales of land, as well as more extensive liberalization, would actually do more to disentangle officialdom and the private sector and to promote de-racketization than would any form of restatization. A crucial distinction must be made between state officials reasserting their control over economic policy, which means purging the government of representatives of private economic interests, and state ownership of or control over economic activity. The former is indeed crucial to de-racketization. The latter is a prescription for corruption, rent-seeking, and economic decline.

If the statist temptation should be shunned and the Asian experience not misinterpreted in economics, so too should the authoritarian temptation be avoided—and again, the Asian experience not misinterpreted—in politics. The state must get back into the business of law enforcement and do so vigorously, as will be discussed below. But reversion to authoritarianism would probably fail to decriminalize the economy or revive economic performance. Everywhere in the post-Communist world where autocrats have maintained or reasserted power, official predation, rather than the formulation of a coherent program for national development, has characterized policy. Where the extent and harshness of authoritarian control have remained at or reverted to Soviet-era levels—namely, in Belarus, Turkmenistan, and Uzbekistan—criminalization may not have proceeded as far as it has in Russia. In the former set of countries, the state's hand has simply remained so heavy and penetrative that basic public order has been preserved and viable private sectors have not emerged at all. Such alternatives, from the standpoint of reducing criminality and improving economic performance, may not furnish especially attractive or viable models for emulation, as will be discussed below. Asian "developmental dictatorships" (or, more charitably, "guided democracies"), though often lauded for providing policymakers with the "insulation" supposedly needed for adequate state autonomy and strong economic performance, also serve as inappropriate models for Russia. The events of 1997 raise the possibility that, perhaps contrary to earlier appearances, contemporary Indonesian and pretransition Thai and Korean economies are or were little less criminalized than the Russian economy. Recent events also may reveal that what are often dubbed Asian models of modernization, at least in their present incarnation, may well have exhausted themselves—and at a level of economic development roughly analogous to that found in contemporary Russia. However one interprets the roots of the Asian crisis, the luster of developmental dictatorship has dimmed considerably, whether as an exemplar of governmental wisdom and rectitude or as a route to sustainable development.

It is clear, however, that states in all Asian countries that experienced substantial economic growth during the past several decades have done a much better job than the post-Soviet Russian state at maintaining elementary public order and guarding the enforcement of property rights and contracts. Their commitment to order and to some semblance of a rule of law in the market, rather than their—probably illusory—autonomy from the pressures of "special interests" and the citizenry in general, created a tolerable climate for investment and thus more propitious conditions for growth. In this limited respect the Asian cases may serve as models for Russia. Russia's escape from the racket will depend in part on its ability to establish rudimentary order without sacrificing the gains in democratization that it realized after the demise of the Communist regime.

Formulating coherent and feasible prescriptions in the sphere of morals and ethics is particularly difficult. Clearly the government's policy—and the Russian intelligentsia's habit—of obsessing over defining the "Russian idea" will do nothing to foster a real sense of national purpose and solidarity. Development of a genuine, healthy patriotism will require major changes in policy and in intellectuals' habits of thinking. Furthermore, the government's current efforts to curtail the activities of foreign religious organizations on Russian soil, while ostensibly designed to "protect" Russian Orthodoxy (and Islam as well) from culturally pernicious competition, recreate under post-Soviet and post-imperial conditions the subordination of the Orthodox Church and Islamic organizations to the state. This is a form of protection that kills. It reconstitutes old dependencies and precludes the revival of traditional Russian religions as autonomous sources of moral and intellectual development and learning. It also retards the emergence of other, alternative forms of religious commitment that could help to constitute ethical bases for social—and therefore economic—interaction and behavior. By undercutting the revival of indigenous religions and thwarting the introduction of mainstream alternatives from abroad that offer potentially civilizing ethical systems, the state ensures, as Durkheim would predict, the growth of "anomic," fanatical religious and political movements based on intolerant, destructive, consummatory ideologies. The prescriptions that follow from this analysis are largely negative: a halt to diversionary, banal, and wasteful efforts to hash out new "conceptions" of the "Russian idea" in policy statements, scholarly journals, and the popular press, as well as an end to enervating state "protection" of Orthodoxy and efforts to shut out "alien" religious organizations. A revival of civic morals and of commitment to the broader community, however, will require more than this handful of prescriptions aimed merely at curtailing blunders, and it will not happen overnight.

Overcoming the debility of societal organizations similarly will not and cannot happen instantaneously. The legacy of near-total statization of associational life in Russia is too salient and strong for a vigorous civil society to emerge within a few years, or even a decade, of Sovietism's demise. Some post-Communist changes, such as the elimination of most restrictions on association and expression, have opened possibilities for an immeasurably stronger and richer autonomous public realm. On the other hand, some post-Communist conditions actually retard organizational development and maturation. Rising unemployment and poverty, for example, undermine organized labor and in some cases drive it back into the arms of management. Offering prescriptions within the realm of societal-organizational change is especially difficult to do without discussing the potential agents of change. Thus, this problem will be pursued in greater depth in the following section, which specifies how and by whom the Russian economy may be pulled from the racket toward the market.

HOW IT MAY BE DONE

By this point it should be clear that the causes of and thus the remedies for Russia's racket economy are essentially political. With the lone, partial exception of the first causal variable (natural resource endowment), the roots of the racket are neither structural nor immutable. Thus, even if the emergence of a "normal" market economy in the near future is virtually impossible to imagine, given strong and capable agents of political change there is no logical reason why Russia cannot make some progress toward de-racketization.

The primary and most obvious agent of change must be the state. But this statement about the state is empty without specification of which state agencies and actors plausibly may be expected to gain the capacity and to possess the will to launch decriminalizing reforms. Many analysts of present-day Russia regard "the regions" and their leaders as the most probable loci of reform and sources of good ideas for improving polity and economy. This view helps explain why regional politics and the new "federalism" have become perhaps the most widely investigated topics among social scientists studying Russia. But as obvious as the growth of importance of local and regional politics may be, major change on the national level must come from national-level state institutions. Indeed, a strong central government is crucial if there is to be an orderly recreation of center-periphery relations that does not simply spawn criminalized regional baronies. What is more, the institutional configuration of power and the strong tradition of centralism in Russia guarantee a supreme role for Moscow in any major reform effort—or in any policy of drift that breeds the criminalization and national malaise now in evidence.

Given the presence of a superpresidential regime, any effective thrust for major reform will probably originate with the chief executive. Superpresidentialism does not provide an ideal institutional basis for progress and it generates its own set of pathologies.[44] Yet the president's dominance of the central government and the weakness of the legislature under the Russian constitution, the extreme difficulty of amending the constitution, and the institutionalization of presidential supremacy via the enormous growth of the executive apparatuses since 1991 mean that the presidency is and will remain the locus of major change, at least in the absence of a convulsion that would alter the regime by extraconstitutional means.[45] Political leadership, including and especially that of the president, is of inestimable importance in Russian politics.[46]

Given these realities, the foremost obstacle to economic deracketization is the demonstrated incapacity or unwillingness of President Yeltsin to act. Yeltsin's infirmity and erratic engagement in politics, his lack of judgment in personnel decisions, and his refusal ever to organize a political party on which he could rely in times of crisis have hollowed out what capacity he once had for effecting major reform. Since 1994, Yeltsin's leadership has amounted to issuing periodic, farcical denunciations of the performance of a government that he himself appoints and occasionally purging his government of a member or a faction in order to restore some equipoise among the oligarchs—some would say bandits—to whom he has entrusted the levers of state power. Remarkably, Yeltsin has played the George Washington, the Abraham Lincoln, and the Ulysses Grant of his country. During 1987-91, he was the founding father and agent of independence; during 1991-93, the guarantor of territorial integrity and the victor in a civil conflict that threatened to rend the nation; and after 1993, the hapless hero of earlier battles who out of weakness, insecurity, and disastrous judgment fell into collaboration with and dependence on rapacious private interests, to the severe detriment of his country. In his "Grant" mode, in which he will clearly remain for the remainder of his tenure in power, Yeltsin blocks the reforms that are necessary for pulling the Russian economy back from full criminalization.

Yeltsin's ineptitude is the bad news. The good news is that a change of presidents could produce a radical political rupture; and such a rupture could—although by no means necessarily would—shift the tide against economic racketization. What is more, democratization is sufficiently advanced in Russia that the likelihood of regular, reasonably free and fair elections happening on schedule is high. Popular preferences generally oppose a return to authoritarianism or the command economy, as was shown by Yeltsin's easy victory over Gennadii Ziuganov in 1996. As virtually every public opinion poll or personal conversation that concerns itself with the subject shows, however, the citizenry is outraged by the criminality and is eager to see major changes.[47] As stated above, the electorate's ability to hold politicians accountable is limited, even in the presence of elections, by the weakness of intermediary organizations. Still, as will be discussed below, the possibility of meaningful change in this sphere cannot be ruled out. In any event, all of the ingredients necessary for major reform via a political rupture brought about by a presidential election are in place.

In order for Russia to have some hope for decriminalizing the economy within the framework of democracy, it must have a president who is both intent upon exercising power within the confines of the law and who is willing and able to coerce. The first requirement proposed here is uncontroversial; the second will rub many liberals, in both the West and Russia, the wrong way. But law without a will to coercion does not make for the rule of law. In Russia, the inability or unwillingness of the state to coerce turned the polity and economy over to the "strongest" private actors—meaning those best able to organize the most daunting coercive power—and left the vast majority of citizens defenseless. Under Russian circumstances, a presidential will to and capacity for coercion is the crucial prerequisite to establishing some semblance of "state autonomy." The first crucial coercive actions must be purging the representatives of the FIGs from the government itself, launching investigations into and legal actions against the behemoths who have used their control over the government to dodge taxes and against the smaller-scale extortionists who distort and cripple so much small business activity, seeking the harshest penalties against the guilty, and drawing up and executing a draconian program to reestablish elementary public order.

Carrying out such measures will require not only a new government, but also refurbished organs of law enforcement. Two sets of new agencies are required. The first is a new bureau of well-paid, well-monitored, spirited criminal investigators. The remade portions of the successor organization to the KGB currently responsible for investigation have demonstrated their exhaustion and incompetence. These agencies must be purged of their deeply corrupt leaders and completely reformed or simply disbanded and replaced with a new agency. Such an agency might bear some resemblance to the U.S. FBI; but given the extent of criminalization in Russia, it would have to be larger in relative terms and its mandate somewhat broader in scope. Second, the police must be restructured. Many police functions in Russia are still carried out by the national police force attached to the interior ministry. This organization is entirely inadequate, at least given its present force levels and technical endowment, to deal with the challenges of post-Soviet criminalization. The president must commit substantial resources to help local officials build well-paid and well-equipped municipal and district-level police forces. If such programs require major new budgetary outlays, then the central government must cut expenditures on activities such as modernizing infrastructure or subsidizing agriculture to pay for them. Such a proposal might seem extreme. But given the rate at which criminalization is undermining tax collection capacity, poisoning the climate for investment, driving capital abroad, and destroying citizens' trust in public authority, if the state does not soon make law enforcement its top priority, within a decade it will have no resources left to commit to any other purpose anyway. Indeed, the reality of this danger is already upon the country and its system of public finance. At any rate, sound and vigorous law enforcement would probably more than pay for itself if it could merely raise the ratio of anticipated to actual tax revenues by, say, 20 percent or reduce the magnitude of capital flight by one-third.

Three sets of institutions that have not been discussed to this point are the legal code itself, the courts, and agencies of public prosecution. Needless to say, such institutions could be greatly improved in Russia. But they are not the main problem. The laws, prosecutors, and judges, despite their many shortcomings, are "there" in Russia; law enforcement is not. The will to enforce the law and the agencies of law enforcement are the problem.

Could the cures proposed here prove worse than the disease? If the president abuses the agencies of coercion by deploying them for political repression and/or if the agencies escape the control of elected politicians entirely, the answer could be yes. But the risk is worth taking. The time has come for advocates of democracy, freedom, and a market economy in Russia to recognize that criminalization has already arrested democratization, given rise to a "freedom" that most citizens cannot enjoy, and created a "market" in which "market forces" do not function.

A number of scenarios for change may be envisaged. As always, real-life experiences furnish better models than abstract constructions based on wish lists. The post-Communist world knows three models of de-racketization. The first, and most unproven, may be dubbed the Kostov model. Under its parade of short-lived governments between 1990 and 1997, most of which were dominated by the (Communist-successor) Socialist Party, Bulgaria reached a degree of criminalization comparable to that found in present-day Russia, though the nature and loci of corruption were somewhat different. But after new elections swept a strong right-center party, the Union of Democratic Forces, into power in the spring of 1997, a dramatic change in the state's commitment to law enforcement took place. The new prime minister (a powerful figure in Bulgaria, which has a parliamentary regime), Ivan Kostov, in alliance with his forceful and uncorrupted interior minister and with the support of the popular, liberal president elected in 1996, Petar Stoyanov, issued a public "declaration of war" against mafia figures and their operations and against large-scale tax evaders more generally. He appointed a government nearly free of officials who had a personal stake in specific enterprises or conglomerates. He shook up personnel throughout the national bureaucracy, revived the previously listless—but, as it turned out, not entirely corrupted—interior ministry, and cleared out nearly all of the previous government's officials responsible for regulating and running state-owned enterprises. He thereby greatly increased the state's independence from economic interests that had corrupted the previous government. Launching ingenious legal reforms that placed severe financial pressure on criminal syndicates and a public relations campaign that included publicly exposing mafia networks and their inner workings, Kostov initiated what may be the region's first anticorruption campaign that actually aimed to fulfill its stated purposes. In this respect, the Bulgarian efforts differed from those regularly announced in Russia, which are trumpeted and directed by officials who would find themselves in prison if the campaigns actually succeeded in their stated aims. The new Bulgarian government faces enormous obstacles and the outcome of its efforts is still highly uncertain. But its experiment represents an intriguing and potentially illuminating example of how a political rupture induced by an election and a change of government can lead abruptly to a sea change in the state's approach to racketization. Interestingly, the Kostov government's commitment to decriminalization has helped it consistently maintain public approval ratings in excess of 50 percent, even as it has aggressively pursued painful economic reforms aimed at introducing fiscal austerity, achieving macroeconomic stabilization, and quickening privatization.[48]

The second path to decriminalization is the Lukashenko model. Named for the Belarussian leader who was elected president in 1994 and who subsequently pushed the polity toward closure and dictatorship, this is the most undemocratic and illiberal way to contravene criminality. Lukashenko followed a simple formula: attack all sources of nonstate economic power and bring them back under state control while thwarting all privatization, and reconstitute the KGB and the police and deploy them, Soviet-style, to repress crime and political opposition alike. This approach has an elegance that many Russian Communists and nationalists deeply appreciate.[49]

The third way is the Luzhkov model, the example created by Moscow's mighty mayor, Iurii Luzhkov. Since consolidating his power over the municipal government in 1993–94, Luzhkov has established a degree of political authority unmatched by any other Russian leader. Luzhkov's strategy for dealing with rackets has combined painstaking cooptation with divide-and-conquer tactics. By early 1996, Luzhkov had established enough power and authority to be able consistently and effectively to offer the large private conglomerates and their armed wings operating in Moscow the choice of either submitting to his own personal "protection" or facing strangulation at the hands of his tax inspectors and municipal police. Unlike the Kostov model, the Luzhkov approach does not aim to liberate markets from political influence or corruption; but neither does it, in contrast with the Lukashenko model, seek to eliminate markets and the private sector. It aims to create a state (or a state within a state). In this it has largely succeeded. The Moscow city government is one of the few public entities in Russia that can at least pretend to forecast its own revenues in advance. In the realm of basic public order, Luzhkov created a special municipal police force, equipped with vehicles, weapons, and officers that are often a match for the other side. When Luzhkov took over the mayoralty from the liberal but corrupt and incompetent Gavriil Popov at the beginning of the post-Communist transition, both the economy and the crime rate were deteriorating in Moscow much more quickly than they were in most of the rest of Russia. By mid-1996, violent crime was in decline in Moscow, and the city had become so attractive a magnet for domestic capital that 80 percent of it resided in Moscow. Nearly all foreign direct investment flowed to Moscow as well. What is more, the economy of Moscow by some estimates grew by 10 percent in 1997 while poverty fell dramatically—Chinese-style trends in a country that as a whole remained mired in stagnation.[50] Western observers argue over whether such feats may be credited even partly to the man who makes Chicago's late Richard Daley look like a hapless administrator and a genial soft touch, but Muscovites themselves are not so divided. In the summer of 1996, 89 percent of the country's most liberal and cosmopolitan electorate voted for Luzhkov's reelection, though Luzhkov faced the opposition of four other ostensibly viable candidates, never bothered to campaign or even announce that he was running again, and engaged in no electoral force or fraud.

The Luzhkov model did not create or even aim to create "clean government." Few Muscovites regard the mayor and his close associates as models of virtue and practitioners of graft-free administration. But fewer still would question that the lion's share of capital the mayor raises and controls is reinvested in the city. As Ian Shapiro notes in an apt distinction, "There is a difference between the kind of corruption where bureaucrats skim a percentage off the top of public projects and the kind in kleptocracies, where they simply consume public revenues and scuttle the projects."[51] The corruption in the Moscow municipal government may amount to more than mere "skimming," but it is organized in a way that allows projects to be carried out and that prevents the emergence of full-blown kleptocracy—a form of system that the national government has indeed begun to approximate. The key to Luzhkov's success is his commitment to building *protective institutions*—namely, a feared police force and an informal, hierarchical network of business interests that all pay him tribute, depend on him for cover, and abide by his orders. Under the Luzhkov administration, the flow and direction of bribes have become more predictable, extortion has become less violent and reduced in scope, competition between conglomerates has become more regularized and more subject to discipline and manipulation by political authorities, and the streets have become safer. A state now exists in Moscow—but it is located in city hall, not in the Kremlin.[52]

Which, if any, of these three paths to de-racketization provides a workable model for Russia, and who might put a viable scheme into practice? The Kostov model would be the most desirable from the standpoint of launching economic decriminalization without reversing democratization. In the abstract, it is not inconceivable that a future Russian president may prove willing and able to pursue such a model. What is more, such an approach might provide not only a framework for reducing racketization, but also for grappling with the second-order, more strictly technical problems discussed above. Indeed, the Kostov government has shown a keen interest not only in de-racketization, but also in launching new efforts in enterprise restructuring and in reconstructing the country's financial institutions. The Kostov approach would be highly consistent with moving Russia toward European norms and practices. From the perspective of a Western liberal or social democrat, it represents both a viable and a highly desirable model for transformation in Russia (as, of course, it does in Bulgaria).

It is nevertheless difficult to imagine who the agents of such a program might be. Russia has no right-center political party that can come close to rivaling Kostov's Union of Democratic Forces in terms of membership magnitude, public support, or organizational coherence and élan. Nor does it have a Kostov—a personally appealing, pragmatic, economically literate, hard-nosed liberal who actually delights in the grind of party-building. Most leading Russian liberals, including Iavlinskii and Gaidar, possess neither the political skills needed for election nor the slightest idea of how to wield coercive power effectively. Chubais and Boris Federov probably have the latter but lack the former. Boris Nemtsov, currently a deputy prime minister, may have the former but probably lacks the latter. Aleksandr Lebed may well possess both. But Lebed's dedication to the market is still uncertain. Furthermore, his support of Aleksandr Korzhakov, the former head of Yeltsin's personal bodyguard and the very personification of official corruption and abuse of power, in the election to fill the parliamentary seat that Lebed vacated during his brief stint in Yeltsin's government in 1996, casts grave doubt on the sincerity of Lebed's self-proclaimed commitment to economic decriminalization and the rule of law.

Lebed may be no Kostov, but nor is he a Lukashenko. Still, the would-be agents of a Lukashenko model are not difficult to find in Russia. They are plentiful among the most unreconstructed of Russia's Communists. The chance of a victory by Gennadii Ziuganov in a future presidential election cannot be ruled out; nor can the possibility that Ziuganov, once in power, would commit himself to Lukashenko-style restoration. Given popular political preferences, however, the victory of Ziuganov or a figure of his ilk is unlikely. What is more, once in office, such a politician would almost certainly find opposition to economic resovietization insurmountable. Lukashenko faced a much simpler challenge in the Belarus of the mid-1990s than any Russian president would at the beginning of the next decade. The powerful conglomerates that control the Russian economy may be tameable, but they probably are not destructible. Any effort directly to annihilate them would provoke massive counterforce and would probably prove futile.

In fact, one may question whether the Lukashenko model is sustainable even in Belarus itself, particularly on the border of an increasingly democratic, prosperous, and powerful Poland. It certainly contains a number of serious drawbacks as a model for emulation in Russia. The model ensures exclusion from Europe and ostracism by the West in general. It spells growing restiveness and burgeoning costs of repression at home. One may also question whether the Lukashenko model really "solves" in any meaningful sense the problem of criminality. By destroying all accountability of the rulers to the ruled and attempting to preserve a command economy, the Lukashenko approach reproduces the underworlds and undergrounds that undergirded the Soviet economic system, which ultimately proved utterly incapable of promoting national prosperity, private responsibility, or public probity. The Lukashenko model also provides scant basis for solving the daunting technical problems that Russia faces, such as creating modern agencies of finance and diversifying production in a manner that reduces dependence on primary production. The Lukashenko model is about reestablishing Soviet-era lines of command, not spurring innovation and institution-building.

The Luzhkov model might prove more workable. One can easily imagine who its agent might be. What is more, it is not difficult to envision the mayor capturing the presidency on the promise that he will accomplish on the national level what he has done in the capital city. Luzhkov may well have the imagination, savvy, and ruthlessness to do so, though his brand of decriminalization would be of a very particular type. He may possess the capability to establish some state autonomy vis-à-vis powerful private interests and to construct and manage reasonably effective agencies of coercion. But a Luzhkov presidency might or might not include a commitment to bolstering the rule of law and building democratic institutions. It also might or might not stimulate creative solutions to economic problems such as diversifying production and modernizing the financial system. Luzhkov's record as mayor does not make possible confident predications on these matters. A Luzhkov presidency certainly could not be expected to contribute to eradicating the fourth and fifth roots of racketization explicated above. In comparative perspective, the state often does play an important role in shaping public morality and fostering a sense of collective purpose.[53] It also frames the incentives that structure the lives of autonomous societal organizations.[54] But if Luzhkov's actions as mayor provide a guide, a Luzhkov government (or one like it) on the national level would not concern itself deeply with revitalizing public morality or with nurturing autonomous societal organizations. These tasks, as well as that of countervailing the possibly authoritarian side effects of official efforts to curb criminalization, would fall to nonstate actors. Indeed, although discussion to this point has focused on the state as the main potential agent of decriminalization, the state alone, even if governed by powerful and well-intentioned figures, cannot possibly eradicate all the roots of the racket. Societal actors will have to contribute a great deal, particularly in the moral and organizational realms, if racketization is to be reversed.

It is not easy to locate in Russian society entities that reasonably may be expected to serve as generators of moral renewal, social cohesion, and group membership. But several potential agents are visible. One is small business and its associations. Economic transformation in Russia has been kindest to certain strata of enterprise managers, the previously well endowed and well connected, and politicians themselves. It has been cruelest to the most vulnerable groups, including pensioners and unskilled laborers living outside the few largest cities. Between these groups, however, is located a stratum of new small entrepreneurs and their employees. This group is sizable: by the end of 1995, 15 percent of the Russian labor force owned or worked in private small business. While indubitably heterogeneous in many ways, it is monolithically opposed to a reversion to authoritarianism and a command economy. Some 96 percent of individuals in this sector supported Yeltsin in his successful run against Ziuganov in the second round of the 1996 presidential election.[55] Whether or not this group might serve as a powerful social counterweight to the "big" industrialists and financiers, in a way that roughly analogous groups did in the nineteenth century (and in some respects do even to the present day) in parts of the West, remains to be seen. This stratum of Russian society is still poorly understood, and its political and economic role is not yet readily discernible.

The second potential group is academics and intellectuals. While the transition erased the social distinctiveness of Soviet-era intelligentsia, intellectuals and academic specialists remain vital and potentially politically relevant members of society. They occupy a peculiar niche insofar as they combine three characteristics that do not always coexist comfortably among other social groups. First, they have clearly "lost" a great deal in strictly economic terms from the transition; second, they may be the best informed and most outraged group in terms of their attitudes toward the racketization of the economy; and third, they clearly support democracy and oppose authoritarian reversion. Academics and intellectuals played a crucial role in changing the moral climate of society and in organizing the groups that helped pushed the Soviet regime to its demise in 1989–91.[56] It would be premature to specify a particular "role" for academics and intellectuals in eradicating the roots of the racket. But given these individuals' economic stations, political orientations, and previous political activity, it would be a mistake to ignore their potential influence.

A third potentially potent source of change is found among providers of public information, specifically professional journalists and employees of think tanks, many of which function at least in part as nonstate public information agencies. This group, like small business, is understudied and poorly understood.[57] The opportunities for the growth of this stratum, membership in which is established by a place in the new system of communicative interaction, originally grew out of the drama of glasnost. In fact, since the realm of communicative interaction opened "early"—during the middle of the Gorbachev period—journalists had something of a head start in the formation of a genuine collective identity. There are several reasons to expect journalists and other providers of public information possibly to develop a special capacity for advancing social integration and even contributing to ethical change. The first is the common identity that has developed among journalists and the extent to which this identity runs deeper than that seen in other occupations. There are no hard data to support such a generalization; it is based on little more than extensive personal observation. Many private media organs are, of course, directly affiliated with one or another FIG, and journalists themselves are scarcely immune from corruption and political pressure. Yet this author's strong impression is that even among journalists of disparate political orientations, there exists a kernel of shared identity based on a mutual sense of responsibility. Perhaps to a greater extent than in the West, many Russian journalists regard themselves not only as providers of information, but also as surrogate social scientists, as interpreters of social reality. This is unsurprising given the decimation of the social sciences as well as of a realm of open communication during the Soviet period, and it need not be seen as a sign of lack of professionalism. Indeed, if Durkheim was correct to define professionalization largely in terms of the development of a shared set of ethics, journalists and other providers of information may now constitute the closest thing post-Soviet Russia has to a genuine profession.[58] What is more, the sense of social cohesion among journalists crosses internal geographical boundaries. One finds the same sense of belonging and the same commitment to public information and education among groups of journalists in Saratov or Orel as one finds in Moscow. When journalists in Tula refer to "us," moreover, they are often referring to their fellows in Moscow and in St. Petersburg no less than to their colleagues in their own locality. Such a cosmopolitan feeling of corporate identity and commitment is uncommon among other groups in post-Soviet Russia. The beginnings of a sense of group membership among providers and interpreters of public information may bode well for the growth of societal counterweights to economic criminalization, all the more so given that journalists often play the role of opposition to the custodians of economic and political power.

Given the daunting transformations of state power and societal organization necessary to move the Russian economy from the racket to the market, thoroughgoing economic decriminalization cannot be regarded as probable, at least not in the near future. Yet the political nature of the roots of the racket economy and the changeability of post-Communist politics mean that breakthroughs are not inconceivable. Stranger things than the decriminalization of the Russian economy—including 7 percent growth rates in Poland, the emergence of a democratic Mongolia, Hungarian membership in NATO, the rise of a Naziphilic dictator in Belarus, and indeed the dissolution of communism itself—have happened during the past decade in the vast Eurasian space in which Russia occupies the central place.

NOTES

Research for this article was supported by funds provided by a Fellowship Grant from the National Council for Eurasian and East European Research, under the authority of a Title VIII Grant from the U.S. Department of State. Neither the Council nor the U.S. government is responsible for its findings or contents. The author would also like to thank Jonah Levy, Gabriella Montinola, and John Zysman for many incisive comments on earlier drafts of this article, and Ivan Ascher for able research assistance.

1. Emile Durkheim, *Professional Ethics and Civic Morals* (New York: Routledge, 1992), p. 96.

2. Theodore Lowi, *The End of Liberalism,* 2d ed. (New York: Norton, 1979), p. 261.

3. To the best of my knowledge, the term "racket economy" was coined with reference to post-Soviet Russia by George W. Breslauer in "Reflections on the Anniversary of the August 1991 Coup," *Post-Soviet Affairs* 8, 2 (1992): 168. On the problem of organized crime in Russia more generally, see, for example, the works of Louise I. Shelley, including "Post-Soviet Organized Crime," *Demokratizatsiya* 2, 3 (Summer 1994): 341–58, and other articles in the same issue; Stephen Holmes, "What Russia Teaches Us Now," *American Prospect* 33 (July–August 1997): 30–39; and Alexei Verizhnikov, "Uncivil Society and Lawlessness-Enforcing Agencies," *Geschichte und Gegenwart* 1 (1997): 43–54.
4. See, for example, Terry Karl, *The Paradox of Plenty: Oil Booms and Petro-States* (Berkeley: University of California Press, 1997).
5. "Oleg Soskovets: 'My ne otkazhemsia ot reform'," *Nezavisimaia gazeta*, 12 March 1996; "Glava gosudarstva podderzhal FPG," *Segodnia*, 2 April 1996; and "Ekonomike strany ne nuzhna politicheskaia likhoradka," *Kommersant*, 27 April 1996. In-depth examination of the FIGs is provided in Juliet Johnson, "Russia's Emerging Financial-Industrial Groups," *Post-Soviet Affairs* 13, 4 (October–December 1997): 333–65.
6. Alexei Zudin, "Business and Politics in Post-Communist Russia." Issued by the Center for Political Technologies, Moscow, 1995. Available at http://www.cipe.org/efn/cpt3.html.
7. See, for example, "Presidenta bol'she net, no kreslo ego ostaetsia," *Kommersant*, 16 October 1996; and "Finansovaia diktatura," *Nezavisimaia gazeta*, 22 October 1996.
8. See "Reforma 'Gazproma' odobrena," *Kommersant*, 16 May 1997; and Zudin.
9. "Finansovaia diktatura," *Nezavisimaia gazeta*, 22 October 1996.
10. Bertrand Russell, *Power* (London: Routledge, 1992), pp. 88–89.
11. Immanuel Kant, *Political Writings*, ed. Hans Reiss (Cambridge: Cambridge University Press, 1995), pp. 105, 117, 134, 195, 231.
12. Vladimir Shlapentokh, "'Normal' Russia," *Current History* 96, 612 (October 1997): 333.
13. Lowi, pp. 36–39. Quoted passage appears on p. 37; emphasis in the original.
14. I am indebted to Edward W. Walker for information and insights on this issue.
15. For an interesting early assessment of Russia's post-Soviet "crisis of values," see B. G. Kapustin, "Krizis tsennostei i shansy rossiiskogo liberalizma," *Politicheskie issledovaniia* 5–6 (1992): 76–83.
16. Ferenc Fehér, Agnes Heller, and György Márkus, *Dictatorship Over Needs* (Oxford: Basil Blackwell, 1983), pp. 208–13.
17. Durkheim, *Professional Ethics and Civic Morals*, p. 14.
18. M. Steven Fish, *Democracy from Scratch: Opposition and Regime in the New Russian Revolution* (Princeton: Princeton University Press, 1995), pp. 106–7.

19. See D. E. Furman, "Massovoe soznanie rossiiskikh evreev i antisemitizm," *Svobodnaia mysl'* 4 (1994): 36–51.

20. I am indebted to Jonah Levy for this apt analogy.

21. Emile Durkheim, *The Division of Labor in Society* (Glencoe, Ill.: Free Press, 1960), pp. 39–46, 70–173.

22. M. Steven Fish, "Russia's Fourth Transition," in *The Global Resurgence of Democracy*, ed. Larry Diamond and Marc F. Plattner, 2d ed., pp. 264–75 (Baltimore: Johns Hopkins University Press, 1996).

23. Gabriella Montinola, "The Efficient Secret Revisited: The Emergence of 'Clean Government' in Chile"; paper presented at the meeting of the Latin American Studies Association, Mexico City, March 1997.

24. M. Steven Fish, "The Predicament of Russian Liberalism," *Europe-Asia Studies* 49, 2 (1997): 214–15.

25. World Bank, *From Plan to Market: World Development Report 1996* (New York: Oxford University Press, 1996), pp. 66–72.

26. I am indebted to Lucan Way for expert analysis and insights on cross-regional variation in Ukraine.

27. Ilya Prizel, "Ukraine between Proto-Democracy and 'Soft' Authoritarianism," in *Democratic Changes and Authoritarian Reactions in Russia, Ukraine, Belarus, and Moldova*, ed. Karen Dawisha and Bruce Parrott, pp. 356–65 (Cambridge: Cambridge University Press, 1997).

28. Many non-Russians of course were included in the leadership of the Communist Party's ruling organs, and anti-Communist Russian nationalists never tire of pointing out that many of the revolution's makers were Jewish and that Stalin was a Georgian. But the party's leadership was always predominantly Russian, all the more so after Stalin consolidated his power. At any rate, I use the term "Russian" here in the sense conveyed by *rossiiskii* rather than *russkii*, meaning "inhabitant of Russia" rather than "ethnic Russian." See Ronald Grigor Suny, *The Revenge of the Past* (Stanford, Calif.: Stanford University Press, 1993), pp. 108–10.

29. For stimulating relevant discussions, see *ibid.*, pp. 155–60; Hélène Carrère d'Encausse, *The End of the Soviet Empire* (New York: Basic Books, 1993), pp. 171–95; Andrei Sinyavsky, *Soviet Civilization* (New York: Little, Brown, 1988), pp. 258–64; and John B. Dunlop, *The Rise of Russia and the Fall of the Soviet Empire* (Princeton: Princeton University Press, 1993), pp. 119–20.

30. See Michael Urban, *The Rebirth of Politics in Russia* (Cambridge: Cambridge University Press, 1997), pp. 262–63.

31. See Andrei Kortunov, "Russia, the 'Near Abroad,' and the West," in *The New Russia*, ed. Gail W. Lapidus, p. 150 and note 8 (Boulder, Colo.: Westview, 1995), and Anders Åslund, *How Russia Became a Market Economy*, (Washington, D.C.: Brookings Institution, 1995), pp. 72–73.

32. Kathryn Hendley, *Trying to Make Law Matter* (Ann Arbor: University of Michigan Press, 1996), pp. 17–34.

33. Many Western liberals, including some nonlibertarians, also hold such a view. See for example, Judith N. Shklar, "The Liberalism of Fear," in *Liberalism and the Moral Life,* ed. Nancy L. Rosenblum, pp. 21–38 (Cambridge, Mass.: Harvard University Press, 1989).

34. On the Russian liberals' attitude toward problems of public order, see Fish, "The Predicament of Russian Liberalism," pp. 208–15 and note 56.

35. Author's notes on remarks of Stephen E. Hanson during a meeting of the working group on "Rebuilding Russia: The Next Phase," at the 37th Strategy for Peace Conference of the Stanley Foundation, Warrenton, Virginia, 24–26 October 1996. Also see Stephen E. Hanson, *Time and Revolution* (Chapel Hill: University of North Carolina Press, 1997).

36. For valuable treatments of economic issues, see, for example, Edward P. Lazear, ed., *Economic Transition in Eastern Europe and Russia* (Stanford, Calif.: Hoover Institution, 1995); Joseph R. Blasi, Maya Kroumova, and Douglas Kruse, *Kremlin Capitalism* (Ithaca: Cornell University Press, 1997); Bartlomiej Kaminski, ed., *Economic Transition in Russia and the New States of Eurasia* (Armonk, N.Y.: M. E. Sharpe, 1996); Barry W. Ickes, Peter Murrell, and Randi Ryterman, "End of the Tunnel?" *Post-Soviet Affairs* 13, 2 (April–June 1997): 105–33; and Juliet Johnson, "Banking in Russia," *Problems of Post-Communism* 43, 3 (May–June 1996): 49–59.

37. See the trenchant analysis in Urban, pp. 296–97.

38. Jadwiga Staniszkis, *The Dynamics of the Breakthrough in Eastern Europe* (Berkeley: University of California Press, 1991), pp. 38–69, 163–69, 205–14.

39. Conversation with Antoni Z. Kaminski, Warsaw, 12 July 1997.

40. M. Steven Fish, "The Determinants of Economic Reform in the Postcommunist World," *East European Politics and Societies* 12, 1 (Winter 1998): 31–78.

41. James Riedel and Bruce Comer, "Transition to a Market Economy in Viet Nam," in *Economies in Transition: Comparing Asia and Eastern Europe,* ed. Wing Thye Woo, Stephen Parker, and Jeffrey D. Sachs, pp. 193–96; quoted passage appears on p. 196 (Cambridge, Mass.: MIT Press, 1997).

42. "Private Party," *Far Eastern Economic Review,* 2 October 1997.

43. See Minxin Pei, "Microfoundations of State-Socialism and Patterns of Economic Transformation," *Communist and Post-Communist Studies* 29, 2 (1996): 131–45; Yuan Zheng Cao, Gang Fan, and Wing Thye Woo, "Chinese Economic Reforms: Past Successes and Future Challenges," in Woo, Parker, and Sachs, eds., pp. 28–39.

44. Eugene Huskey, "The State-Legal Administration and the Politics of Redundancy," *Post-Soviet Affairs* 11, 2 (April-June 1995): 115–43; M. Steven Fish, "The Pitfalls of Russian Superpresidentialism," *Current History* 96, 612 (October 1997): 326–30.

45. In my own view, the chances of constitutional amendment that would significantly alter the formal distribution of power in Russia are remote, but some experts on constitutionalism in Russia might disagree with this

opinion. For a thorough and incisive analysis that offers a less skeptical assessment of the chances for change in this crucial realm, see Robert Sharlet, "The Politics of Constitutional Amendment in Russia," *Post-Soviet Affairs* 13, 3 (July–September 1997): 197–227.

46. See George W. Breslauer and Catherine Dale, "Boris Yel'tsin and the Invention of a Russian Nation-State," *Post-Soviet Affairs*, 13, 4 (October–December 1997), pp. 303–32.

47. "Bud' proshche—i k tebe potianutsia liudi," *Kommersant*, 18 July 1995.

48. For relevant articles on Bulgaria, see Krassen Stanchev, "Will Democratic Government Fight Corruption?," *Institute for Market Economics Newsletter* (Sofia) 4, 7–8 (July–August 1997); and "Ministry Will Reform Courts from Within," "Alexander Bozhkov: 'There Is a Change for the Better'," and "Interior Ministry Performs Unprecedented Drug Arrests," *Sofia Independent*, 9–15 January 1998. A rough and as of now even less proven, but nevertheless remarkable and highly salient, analogy to the Kostov case is the new government of Kim Dae-Jung in South Korea. As of this writing, Kim, like Kostov, appears to be genuinely intent upon assaulting the ties and networks that link politicians to big business and to doing so within the framework of a nonpopulist effort that deploys state power to free market forces from the distortions induced by corruption. See "President-Elect Kim Says 'No Government Interference' in Banks," *Korea Times*, 10 February 1998, and "President-Elect Kim Announces Lineup of Senior Secretaries," *Korea Times*, 11 February 1998.

49. On Belarus, see Kathleen J. Mihalisko, "Belarus: Retreat to Authoritarianism," in Dawisha and Parrott, eds., pp. 252–77.

50. Marshall I. Goldman, "Russia's Reform Effort: Is There Growth at the End of the Tunnel?," *Current History* 96, 612 (October 1997): 315–16.

51. Ian Shapiro, *Democracy's Place* (Ithaca, N.Y.: Cornell University Press, 1996), p. 87. Assessing the extent of corruption more precisely is, of course, a daunting and elusive task under any circumstances. For the beginnings of an ambitious effort to do so, see Thomas D. Lancaster and Gabriella R. Montinola, "Toward a Methodology for the Comparative Study of Political Corruption," *Crime, Law, and Social Change* 27 (1997): 185–206.

52. For a telling report on Luzhkov that summarizes highlights from a rare press conference given by him, see Philippa Fletcher, "Moscow Mayor Attacks Russian Government Reformers," *Reuters News Service*, Moscow, 15 January 1998.

53. Durkheim, *Professional Ethics and Civic Morals*, pp. 47–54, 68–70; Lowi, pp. 267–68; Sheldon Garon, *Molding Japanese Minds: The State in Everyday Life* (Princeton: Princeton University Press, 1997).

54. Fish, *Democracy from Scratch*, pp. 72–77, 80–199.

55. "NG—Stsenarii," *Nezavisimaia gazeta*, 29 June 1996.

56. See Marc Garcelon, "The Estate of Change: The Specialist Rebellion and the Democratic Movement in Moscow, 1989–91," *Theory and Society* 26 (1997):

39–85; Richard Rose, Evgeny Tikhomirov, and William Mishler, "Understanding Multi-Party Choice: The 1995 Duma Election," *Europe-Asia Studies* 49, 5 (1997): 807, 814–15.

57. The recent appearance of some high-quality studies bodes well for overcoming this deficit. Particularly noteworthy is Ellen Michiewicz, *Changing Channels: Television and the Struggle for Power in Russia* (New York: Oxford University Press, 1997).

58. Durkheim, *Professional Ethics and Civic Morals*, pp. 14–27.

APPENDIX

ENLARGING EUROPE: THE INDUSTRIAL FOUNDATIONS OF A NEW POLITICAL REALITY

Edited by John Zysman and Andrew Schwartz[1]

SUMMARY

Europe's political boundaries are being redrawn by the enlargement of the European Union (EU) and the extension of the North Atlantic Treaty Organization (NATO), while the continent's industrial fabric is being rewoven by myriad decisions about investment and trade. Political imperatives, not calculations of possible economic gains, have dictated the decision to enlarge the EU. Given those political imperatives, the essays in *Enlarging Europe* consider the industrial integration of the Central and East European countries (CEECs) into the broader European economy, a twin process of transformation in the East and structural adaptation in the West. The way in which the industrial fabric of Europe is rewoven will certainly have far-reaching political significance. Most economists would contend that the real extent of the probably positive adjustments is so limited that the appropriate policy is to soldier on through the admissions process. Political analysts note that the dislocations and the fears they engender among key electorates are giving rise to radical political movements which have the potential to disrupt established political regimes. Those concerned with Europe maintain that the admission of a large number of poorer countries risks changing the policy coalitions and the policy mechanics of the EU. The view presented in *Enlarging Europe,* which begins with the industrial developments that have already begun to link East and West, suggests at least the outlines of a future trajectory in which Eastern industrial development fosters Western prosperity and employment. This alternate perspective requires that we begin our discussion by situating Europe's adaptation to an evolving global economy.

Part I of the book, "Europe Adapting to a World Economy: The New Dynamics," argues that the competitive conditions to which Europe must adapt are not exclusively European. At the end of the twentieth century, Eastern Europe is reentering an international economy very different from the one it left just after World War II. New corporate strategies, hiding behind code words such as "globalism," have changed the terms of industrial competition and induced the rapid evolution of international production networks (IPNs). Based on an analysis of the new terms of global competition, the book spells out the nature of the competitive challenge for Europe today.

Production Networks and the New Terms of Industrial Competition. In their contribution, Michael Borrus and John Zysman explain the significance of two interrelated phenomena, the rise of "Wintelism" and the emergence of IPNs, both with roots in American technology competition and which, taken together, are altering the terms of competition in global markets.

The Strategic Innovation. "Wintelism" is the code word created to suggest the dominance of the *Windows* operating system and *Intel*'s domination of the evolution of microprocessors. It signifies the shift in competition away from final assembly and vertical control of markets by final assemblers. The key notion is that the ability of a firm to exercise market power moves from branding or simple production cost and quality to control over the market through product standards.

An important consequence is that product advantage in markets for critical systems elements is often held through product standards in the form of intellectual property, not by trade secrets embedded in production or defended through the very rapid evolution of product. For example, control of the market does not turn as critically on the distinctive internal mastery of the production process and assembly as was the case with Henry Ford's mass production or Toyota's "lean" production innovations. Factors more essential are speed to market, agility in the adjustment of product features, and the ability to draw on the innovative capacities of particular nodes in the networks.

The Tactical Counterpart. The shift in strategy and competitive dynamics alters how a firm exerts market control and attacks the market. The IPN is the organizational counterpart to Wintelism. IPNs are relationships among firms that organize, across national borders, research and development, product definition and design, procurement, distribution, manufacturing, and support services in a given industry. IPNs, whether internally managed by multinational corporations (MNCs) or animated by contract manufacturers providing a production service, have turned large segments of complex manufacturing into a commodity available in the market. Formerly vertically integrated assemblers such as IBM, Hewlett-Packard, and Apple have disposed of captive production facilities—that is, the facilities they themselves own and operate—and moved to extensive contracting. These moves allow firms to concentrate on design and the reorganization of marketing and distribution operations while conserving capital and gaining flexibility.

IPNs now touch the core elements of the industrial economy and the most innovative and rapidly expanding sectors. Wintelism and IPNs as a potent strategic combination are most evident in the electronics industry, but the approach is of general importance across a set of industries, such as automobiles. It is spreading as an idea, a conception of how to proceed, that is often promoted through popular press versions such as the "virtual corporation" and by the availability of manufacturing service companies that provide production on a contract basis.

The Nature of the Competitive Challenge for Europe. The contribution by Constanze Kurz and Volker Wittke contrasts two basic ways in which European firms are using Eastern producers as part of their production networks: the *least cost* and the *complementary specialization* strategies. The least cost strategy consists of moving existing production arrangements to a lower-wage location. At the same time, the low wage nodes in the Višegrad countries have quickly adapted to more expanded roles that take advantage of their skills. In Asia, similarly, even these limited starting points permitted producers, and countries, to learn, invest, and move up market. Transfer to low-wage locations, of course, involves relatively little effort to plan and prepare. It is a relatively straightforward strategy for West European firms faced with high domestic costs. Consequently, these kinds of moves take place first and fastest.

The pools of existing East European skills already permit a second strategy, however: complementary specialization. It draws on the special skills of the Eastern producers or organization of low-cost skilled work to create distinctive industrial capacities. The stated objective for both Skoda (Volkswagen) and ABB is to offer Western quality and technology at Eastern costs. Because developing strategies of complementary specialization requires longer planning and indeed greater operational certainty, the planning period has lasted longer and is only now taking full effect. For many European firms the Asian experience serves as a guide. Corporations across Europe, especially in Germany, are moving aggressively to take advantage of the more heterogeneous production environment created by the larger Europe to reconsider and reorganize their production strategies.

Part II, "Networks: Experiments and Experimentation," reviews the empirical evidence on the ongoing Central and East European (CEE) trajectory of industrial development, exploring the emergence of IPNs in Europe as a response to the region's new heterogeneity. After an initial pattern of low-cost, low-value-added outward processing trade (OPT) with Western Europe, the CEECs are increasingly turning toward a more sophisticated and more promising developmental model based on complementary reorganization of production in an increasingly integrated regional economy. The East European producers do not have, by and large, the management and technical skills to compete with MNCs; most cannot provide the quality of production and certainty of delivery required to be first-tier suppliers. Moreover, the East European economies for the most part do not have the physical infrastructure (for instance, communications, transportation, financial services) to support effective and rapid development of indigenous world class firms. Consequently, their positions in supply networks organized and maintained by European, American, and Asian MNCs may prove critical.

The Beginning of Network Experimentation and the Demand for Network Participants. While a process of experimentation and development is just beginning, it is improbable that initial developments will be good predictors of final patterns. Nonetheless, the available evidence suggests that the initial elements of at least some form of European IPNs are being put into place, which implies that a steady development toward network-based production is possible.

Aggregate Trade and Industry Data. Michael A. Landesmann shows that recent East-West European trade data indicate a marked increase in vertical intra-industry trade, far greater in fact than the already rapid expansion in regional trade as a whole. Indeed for Hungary, the Czech Republic, and Slovenia, with Poland close behind, indices of intra-industry trade are already higher than in countries like Portugal and Greece. Intra-industry trade is exchange within a supply chain in which producers representing diverse packages of wages and technical skills form part of the production network. Suggested in a variety of ways—by wage rate differentials, productivity differentials, and unit value of traded goods—such trade flows represent tell-tale evidence of the emergence of complex IPNs.

Beneath these broad aggregate trends for the CEE area as a whole, Paolo Guerrieri finds divergent patterns of export and production specialization among the CEECs. Some countries, such as the Czech Republic, Hungary, Poland, and to some extent Slovakia, have engaged in substantial restructuring of their economies, while others are much less advanced on the path of reform. To a varying degree, however, all CEECs still clearly lag behind the West European pack, as shown by their lack of competitiveness in both specialized-suppliers and science-based goods.

As Françoise Lemoine shows in her contribution, in the early 1990s OPT drove CEE exports, accounting for nearly 20 percent of total EU imports in 1992. Movement in the direction of more complex networks with more extensive local technological contribution is underway in the more advanced Central European countries: Hungarian industry is already substantially internationalized, while internationalization is well under way in Poland and the Czech Republic. The data on both foreign direct investment (FDI) and trade indicate that IPNs, though still in their infancy, are increasingly becoming a part of the reconstitution of the European economy.

Industry Case Studies. From a different vantage point, the reorientation of trade away from the Council of Mutual Economic Assistance (CMEA) is intertwined with a reorganization of Western production chains and Eastern entrance into them. Sectoral analyses uncover the logic of the networks that lie behind the trade data. For example, in their case study of the auto industry, Rob van Tulder and Winfried Ruigrok depict the reorganization and reconsideration of the value chains through a mix of least cost production, transfer of existing production to lower cost sites, and "complementary specialization." West European auto companies are increasingly developing products for the East European market that will serve the bottom end of the global market. This is a shift away from the tendency simply to adapt for the East models that have been phased out in the West. Moreover, Western firms are now encouraging suppliers to move East with them.

In textiles and apparel the move East has been led by the Germans and Italians. With the emphasis on low-wage production, OPT arrangements initially played an important role, but FDI has begun to be favored for the Višegrad countries. In his examination of Italian firms' OPT and FDI in the textile and clothing industry, Giovanni Graziani shows that OPT arrangements have been moved further East as wages have risen. Italian clothing manufacturers are starting to revise their perception of local subcontractors, acknowledging the improvement in their quality level through learning, and increasingly relying on them for the supply of complex and high-quality products. A similar process is evident in the furniture and upholstery industries, where 50 percent of German production now comes from German factories in Poland.

In electrical equipment, appliances, and electronics, the processes of reorganization have been slower. Greg Linden's study of the electronics sector suggests that in most cases advanced engineering is kept in the West while skilled production, albeit lower-wage skilled production, is moved East. Moreover, there are hints that nodes of local activity are emerging. System clusters of related activities have emerged, including PCs in the Czech Republic, hard disk drives and audio-visual equipment in Hungary; televisions, washing machines, and batteries in Poland; and lighting equipment and refrigerators in Hungary.

Finally, in the agriculture and food sectors, IPNs are also developing between West and East European producers. Tim Josling and Stefan Tangermann argue that contrary to the fears of the farm sector in Western Europe, the comparative advantage of Eastern agriculture is not in raw materials that are in oversupply in the West. Thus, West European FDI tends to concentrate in highly processed foods with low raw material content. Investment and linkages in the Eastern food processing sectors can indirectly benefit the Western farm sector by fostering more consumer-responsive markets in the CEECs.

Part III, "Policies and Choices, East and West," explores the implications of these economic developments for Europe's competitiveness in global markets and the political and strategic evolution of the region. If the EU fails to seize the opportunity of EU enlargement for developing coherent competitive strategies, the process of EU enlargement will create enormous political and economic difficulties. But if it succeeds, the EU can both improve the competitiveness of its industry in world markets and reinforce the continent's political stability and regional security.

The post-cold-war architecture of Europe is now being constructed. But the external threats against which it would protect are ambiguous and the domestic strategies for growth that it might facilitate are unclear. Steve Weber and John Zysman argue that the complementarity of security and economic means and objectives has come to an end. There are now visible economic prices, such as market access and subsidy, to pay for security objectives. Europe must provide market access and development assistance to the CEECs in an era of high unemployment and demands to reduce state budgets. The problem is not simply the difficulty of defining a security doctrine in the absence of a single clear threat, but rather that there is no clear policy solution to the economic problems and no clear coalition to support it. As a result, the question of costs, both direct budget costs and the indirect costs of accelerated economic adjustment, have become central to the debate on the reintegration of Western and Eastern Europe.

One version of the story of industrial adjustment is that Eastern Europe is a huge pool of low-cost labor, often low-cost *skilled* labor, that threatens both Western jobs that might move East and wages of Western workers who must compete with Eastern production. Seen as market rivals that force economic adaptation or require subsidy, the East European producers represent threats to Western interests that raise the political costs of creating a new regional architecture for Europe. *Enlarging Europe* presents an alternative version of the story. Examining IPNs suggests that Eastern producers may become complements to Western production, permitting the competitive reorganization of European production that defends market position and jobs in global markets.

IPNs and the Opportunity for a New European Bargain. Certainly Europe's objectives toward the East will be more modest than Germany's toward its own reintegration and, hence, less costly. Nonetheless, the gap is enormous; there is a radical divergence between rich Europe and its less developed partners that would now join the community. In absolute terms, measured by percent of GDP, the costs of the disparities may at first glance appear low. But the costs press immediately on the budgets of the EU and more generally contribute to the sense of "global" dislocation that mobilizes political resistance. Certainly the disparities also complicate the governance of the EU.

One consequence of incorporating significant disparities within the Community would be abandoning the notion that, except for temporary delays, the European countries would move forward together. Drawing an analogy between EU enlargement and the emerging geometry of Economic and Monetary Union, Jean Pisani-Ferry sets out the possibility of a *Europe au menu,* wherein the member-states will be able to pick and choose their preferred pace of integration based on a restricted menu of options and a common understanding that each country has a vocation to eventually graduate to the next level of integration. Helen Wallace's chapter suggests, however, that although the "deep" integration model apparently prevails over the "shallow" model in European discourse, it will probably be extremely difficult to construct the political and economic bargains necessary to implement the adjustments demanded by deep integration. In the meantime, misguided strategies on the part of EU governments are likely to persist. Alain Henriot and András Inotaï review several telling examples of this confusion. They note that the spectacular increase in trade flows between the EU and the CEECs since the beginning of the 1990s has fueled a highly politicized debate over industrial de-localization, especially in France and Germany. The sensitivity of public opinion about this issue has made it difficult to facilitate access to EU markets for CEE products.

The risk for the East in this story is equally clear and, in fact, symmetric to that faced by Western Europe. Production organized by Western companies may remain limited to a series of Eastern enclaves isolated from the rest of Eastern economies, rather than the foundations of broad and sustainable growth. As Ellen Comisso demonstrates in her contribution, the national variations in basic strategies for privatization, stabilization, price and trade liberalization, and industrial growth constitute "implicit" development strategies that will determine different market outcomes, including patterns of attachment to the West.

On the positive side, there are important reasons for hope. In their analysis of the economic situation of Eastern Europe, Barry Eichengreen and Richard Kohl argue that the East European countries will most likely approximate the "Iberian model" of economic integration into the EU. In the case of Iberia, the decision to enter the EU was essentially a decision to adopt the rules and market conditions of the advanced countries, to adopt the goal of converging toward a homogeneous European economy rather than a deliberate attempt to insert local producers into a regional division of labor. The authors are optimistic that the convergence of the CEECs with the EU economies will be possible, especially if they avoid social market policies which induce economic rigidities. There is also growing evidence of transition and network experimentation in complex manufacturing that goes beyond OPT arrangements. Although most of it remains concentrated in a handful of the Eastern countries and is being conducted most extensively by German firms, Niels Mygind's contribution suggests that countries that are on the periphery of the CEE area, such as the Baltic economies, are also beginning to experience economic internationalization. Finnish and Swedish investors, in particular, are in the process of establishing international production networks, especially in Estonia.

If one views the East European countries as a source of migrants or products that intensify the pressures for structural adjustment in the West, then the tradeoffs between economics and security will be accentuated. But the Eastern countries also represent an opportunity to orchestrate a finer division of labor that can contribute to the competitive position of the European region as a whole. The division of labor possible as a result of the heterogeneity provided by the East may not only help keep production in Europe, but also permit new production that might not have been considered. In this case, conflicts between security and economic objectives would be muted. The *very disparities that create or at least amplify tensions between*

Europe's regions may also represent a heterogeneity of production functions that contributes to their solution. Much thus turns on the character of the transition away from socialist economic systems and the adaptation and reorganization it brings—that is, on how CEE firms become inserted into the European division of labor.

NOTES

1. A companion volume to this one and part of the BRIE/Kreisky Forum Project on Uniting the European Economy. Published by International and Area Studies, Berkeley, 1998. This summary was prepared with assistance from Nicholas Jabko.

NOTES ON CONTRIBUTORS

Stephen S. Cohen *is Co-Director of BRIE and Professor of City and Regional Planning at the University of California at Berkeley.*

Andrew Schwartz *is a Research Associate at BRIE and a doctoral candidate in the Department of Political Science at the University of California at Berkeley.*

John Zysman *is Co-Director of BRIE and Professor of Political Science at the University of California at Berkeley.*

Manuel Castells *is Professor of City and Regional Planning at the University of California at Berkeley.*

M. Steven Fish *is Associate Professor of Political Science at the University of California at Berkeley.*

Gregory Grossman *is Professor of Economics Emeritus at the University of California at Berkeley.*

Peter Huber *is a Research Assistant at the Austrian Institute of Economics Research, Vienna.*

Andreas Wörgötter *is Head of the Department of Economics at the Institute for Advanced Studies, Vienna.*

INSTITUTE OF INTERNATIONAL STUDIES

POLICY PAPERS IN INTERNATIONAL AFFAIRS

42. *Beware the Slippery Slope: Notes Toward the Definition of Justifiable Intervention.* Ernst B. Haas. $6.50
43. *Industrial Policy Supporting Economic Transition in Central-Eastern Europe: Lessons from Slovenia.* Tea Petrin. $6.95
44. *Small Business Policy in Japan and the United States: A Comparative Analysis of Objectives and Outcomes.* Yuko Aoyama and Michael B. Teitz. $8.25

CENTERS FOR SOUTH AND SOUTHEAST ASIA STUDIES

MONOGRAPH SERIES

33. *Indonesian Transmigrants and Adaptation: An Ecological Anthropological Perspective.* Oekan S. Abdoellah. $14.95
34. *Thai Music and Musicians in Contemporary Bangkok.* Pamela Myers-Moro. $22.50
35. *In the Shadow of Change: Images of Women in Indonesian Literature.* Tineke Hellwig. $22.00

OCCASIONAL PAPERS

16. *Patterns of Migration in Southeast Asia.* Ed. Robert R. Reed. $19.50
17. *Bridging Worlds: Studies on Women in South Asia.* Ed. Sally J. M. Sutherland. $17.50
18. *Essays on Southeast Asian Performing Arts: Local Manifestations and Cross-Cultural Implications.* Ed. Kathy Foley. $14.95
19. *Critical Issues in Philippine Research: A Selected and Annotated Literature Review on the Women's Movement, Conflict in Luzon's Cordillera, Muslim Autonomy, and Recent Political Resistance.* James N. Anderson, Robert R. Reed, and Gaspar L. Sardalla. $25.00

LANGUAGE TEACHING MATERIALS

Introduction to Hindi Grammar. Usha Jain. $35.00

Hmong for Beginners. Annie Jaisser et al. $28.00

Devavanipravesika: Introduction to the Sanskrit Language. Robert P. Goldman and Sally J. Sutherland. $23.50

Teaching Grammar of Thai. William Kuo. $23.50

Tamil for Beginners, 2 vols. Kausalya Hart. $15.00 ea.

SINO-TIBETAN ETYMOLOGICAL DICTIONARY AND THESAURUS PROJECT

MONOGRAPH SERIES

1A. *Bibliography of the International Conferences on Sino-Tibetan Languages and Linguistics I-XXV,* 2d ed. Randy J. LaPolla and John B. Lowe. $28.00

2. *Languages and Dialects of Tibeto-Burman.* Ed. James Matisoff. $20.00

3. *Phonological Inventories of Tibeto-Burman Languages.* Ed. Ju Namkung. $35.00